HOW TO TRANSFORM SUCCESS

A Practical Guide to Navigating the New Era of Impactful Entrepreneurship

DR. SHYAM VASUDEVA RAO

STARDOM BOOKS

www.StardomBooks.com

STARDOM BOOKS

112 Bordeaux Ct.

Coppell, TX 75019, USA

FIRST EDITION MAY 2025

STARDOM BOOKS, LLC.
112 Bordeaux Ct. Coppell, TX 75019, USA

www.stardombooks.com
Stardom Books, United States
Stardom Alliance, India

HOW TO TRANSFORM SUCCESS

A Practical Guide to Navigating the New Era of Impactful Entrepreneurship

DR. SHYAM VASUDEVA RAO

Pages. 272
cm. 13.5 X 21.5
Category: BUS025000 Business & Economics: Entrepreneurship
BUS107000 Business & Economics: Personal Success
SEL027000 Self-Help: Personal Growth - Success

ISBN: 978-1-957456-71-3

DEDICATION

This book is dedicated to my father, who has always been my pillar of strength, protector, and best friend. I am forever grateful to have you in my life.

Contents

ACKNOWLEDGMENTS

The world is a better place because of those who are dedicated to developing and leading others. It becomes even greater when people generously share their time to mentor future leaders. Thank you to everyone who strives to grow and helps others grow along the way.

To all the individuals I have had the privilege to lead, be led by, or observe from afar, your leadership has been an inspiration and a foundation for humanity. I am deeply grateful.

This book would not exist without the experiences and support of my peers and team at my startups. You have given me the opportunity to lead an incredible group of individuals. To be a leader of great leaders is a privilege and a blessing.

Transforming an idea into a book is as complex as it sounds—both an internal challenge and a deeply rewarding experience. I want to extend my heartfelt gratitude to those who made this possible. Special thanks to the incredible team at Stardom: Raam Anand, Ranjitha, Priyadarshini, and Chaya.

Special thanks to my wife Jyothi for not only being a continuous support but also reviewing the contents of this book.

Finally, to my wonderful family—Amma, Jyothi, Vishnu, Vasudev, Anjali, Anna, and little Raghav, my siblings Sunder and Padma Sridhar—thank you for your unwavering love and support.

PREFACE

Historically, success has been measured by wealth, power, and individual achievement, focusing on how much one could accumulate, whether in money, status, or possessions. However, today, success is evolving into something far more inclusive, where purpose, empathy, and societal impact hold equal, if not greater, significance. This shift lies at the core of Transforming Success: Navigating the New Era of Impactful Entrepreneurship.

Reflecting on my entrepreneurial journey, I am reminded of the twists and turns, the triumphs and setbacks that have shaped me. Over time, I've understood that while personal achievement is essential, true success is defined by contributing to something larger than oneself. This book is about redefining success—aligning individual goals with a broader purpose, creating ecosystems that uplift others, and ensuring that the businesses we build leave a lasting, positive impact on the world. This alignment with a larger purpose brings a profound sense of fulfillment, inspiring us to strive for more than personal gain.

I have been driven by a desire to innovate, create, and solve problems since the start of my career. Technology has always fascinated me, particularly its potential to be harnessed for the greater good. Early on, I realized that entrepreneurship—especially in social innovation—was not just about bringing a product to market; it was about addressing real, pressing needs in healthcare, environmental sustainability, and social equity. This drive to merge innovation with impact led me down unexpected paths, from working on groundbreaking healthcare technologies to developing sustainable business models that empower communities. Yet, through all these ventures, one truth has remained constant: success is not measured by the size of a company or the profits it generates but by the lives it touches and the positive change it creates.

Growing up as the eldest sibling, I often played the caretaker role. Whenever one of my brothers or sisters fell ill, I was responsible for taking them to the doctor. I vividly remember those visits—how a doctor could transform a crying, sick child into a smiling one in mere minutes. The magic of medicine fascinated me. The ability of a doctor to directly impact someone's life in such a tangible way stayed with me, sparking an internal conflict. My passion for electronics was unwavering, yet I couldn't help but wonder, Is being a hardware engineer enough? Can I make a difference in the world like these doctors do?

As this question lingered, I began reflecting more deeply on my desired impact. I realized that making a difference wasn't limited to medicine. Engineers, lawyers, and accountants—all professionals—could create meaningful change if they applied their skills toward a greater purpose. I didn't have to abandon my passion for electronics to contribute to the world; I simply needed to channel it in a way that aligned with my desire to make a difference.

This realization was liberating. Until then, much of my drive had been fueled by comparison—competing with others, striving to surpass their achievements. However, as my perspective shifted, success became less about outpacing someone else and more about finding a path aligned with my values and vision for contributing to society.

This alignment, I discovered, is a source of immense empowerment, inspiring me to pursue my goals with renewed vigor and determination.

For years, I had viewed my interests in medicine and electronics as separate, parallel paths that would never intersect. On one hand, I was captivated by electronics—the innovation, design, and potential to create something new. On the other hand, I was deeply moved by how doctors transformed lives through empathy and skill. I often wondered whether my passion for electronics could offer the same level of tangible, life-changing impact. This internal struggle persisted for years as I wrestled with reconciling these two seemingly distinct passions.

However, as I delved deeper into both fields, I began to see that my passions weren't at odds—they were, in fact, complementary. I didn't have to choose between them. Instead, I could integrate them into a single pursuit aligned with my goals and values. This realization was empowering. Innovation and technology weren't confined to the tech sector; they had the potential to revolutionize healthcare. By combining my expertise in electronics with my desire to improve lives, I could carve out a unique space where my skills could solve real-world problems.

Yet, understanding this was only half the battle. The true challenge lay in transforming my mindset. Throughout my early career, I had been conditioned to equate success with climbing the corporate ladder, gaining peer recognition, and securing high-paying, prestigious jobs. Anything outside this traditional framework seemed risky, even irresponsible. However, as I started questioning these assumptions, I realized I needed to break away from conventional career expectations to create the change I envisioned.

I had to let go of the belief that success meant staying within the safety of established institutions. Instead, I embraced uncertainty and took ownership of my path. Becoming an entrepreneur wasn't just a career decision but a complete mindset shift. It required me to think differently, step beyond what was familiar and safe, and take control of my future. This shift in mindset is empowering, giving us the courage to step out of our comfort zones and take charge of our destinies.

Eventually, I chose entrepreneurship as the avenue to merge my passions and make a meaningful impact. As an entrepreneur, I was no longer confined to predefined roles and functions. I could innovate, explore unconventional solutions, and harness my creativity to address healthcare challenges. Entrepreneurship allowed me to build something new—a business model, a product, a solution—based on my unique vision and driven by a desire to make a difference. It offered the opportunity to experiment, fail, learn, and iterate—possibilities that corporate environments often restrict.

Most importantly, entrepreneurship gave me a platform to create a lasting impact. In a corporate setting, I often felt like a cog in the wheel, contributing to significant projects but constrained by the organization's priorities and agendas. As an entrepreneur, I could focus on what mattered most: solving healthcare challenges and making technology accessible to underserved communities. My work wasn't just about scaling a product for profit but about democratizing healthcare and providing the most needed solutions.

This shift in perspective—from seeing myself as just an engineer to embracing the role of a problem-solver and change-maker—was transformative. It required me to develop new skills in leadership, empathy, resilience, and business.

The entrepreneurial journey is full of challenges, but it is deeply gratifying because each step is aligned with a larger mission. Every setback became an opportunity to refine my approach, strengthening my commitment to my vision.

This evolution in my thinking didn't happen overnight. It was a gradual process shaped by experience, reflection, and a growing awareness of the world around me. I began to see that entrepreneurship wasn't just about solving technical problems or bringing innovative products to market. It was about understanding the human side of those problems—the people affected, the communities in need, and the long-term impact of the solutions we create. This expanded vision showed me that success isn't just a personal achievement; it's about contributing to something greater and building a legacy that benefits others.

Today's entrepreneurs are experiencing a fundamental shift in their responsibilities. In the past, profit was the primary focus. Now, modern entrepreneurs are being called to consider the broader impact of their businesses. This shift is especially evident among the next generation of leaders, who are driven by aspirations for success and a deep commitment to making the world a better place.

In this new paradigm, entrepreneurs must be more than businesspeople. They must be social innovators, prepared to tackle the world's most pressing challenges—climate change, healthcare access, and economic inequality. These are not easy problems to solve, but they are essential to building a sustainable and inclusive future.

I am optimistic about entrepreneurship's potential to shape a more equitable and sustainable world. However, to achieve this vision, we must rethink what it means to be an entrepreneur.

We must move beyond the narrow focus on profit and competition and embrace a new model driven by empathy, purpose, and a commitment to social impact.

In "How to Transform Success", I aim to inspire and equip the next generation of entrepreneurs with the tools and mindset they need to succeed in this new era. Whether you are just starting your entrepreneurial journey or looking to pivot toward more meaningful work, this book is for you. Together, we can create a future where success is measured by financial gain and our positive impact on the world.

This is my story, and I hope it inspires you to embark on your journey. The road ahead may not be easy, but I assure you—it will be worth it.

1

RETHINKING SUCCESS

"Try not to become a man of success, but rather try to become a man of value."

–Albert Einstein

I n a world where wealth and material possessions have long been the standard measure of success, have we misunderstood what it truly means to succeed?

When you hear the word success, what comes to mind? Money? A lavish lifestyle? A countryside home perched on the edge of a cliff? Or does it mean something entirely different—perhaps sacrificing for your family, giving back to a society that has shaped you, or supporting a community that desperately needs you?

What general parameters do you use to measure success in your life? Is it the accumulation of material possessions as you climb the socio-economic ladder? Or is the social status and recognition that comes with crossing a certain achievement threshold? The conventional notion of success, often tied solely to financial wealth, requires a profound transformation.

This shift is not just about redefining success but completely reimagining it. It's about freeing ourselves from rigid societal expectations and defining success on our terms.

The Collins Dictionary defines success as: "Someone or something successful achieves a high position, makes a lot of money, or is admired a great deal."

While this definition captures one aspect of success, it also imposes a limited and narrow perspective. It equates success primarily with status, wealth, and external validation, overlooking deeper, more personal measures such as fulfillment, happiness, and impact. True success is far more expansive—it should be an inclusive concept that embraces diverse aspirations and achievements beyond traditional metrics.

Success should be about fully leveraging our potential, nurturing meaningful relationships, and embracing a sense of purpose. But it doesn't end there. True success also involves positively impacting society through volunteering, philanthropy, mentorship, or leaving a lasting, positive legacy. This broader, more holistic perspective recognizes that success is not a one-size-fits-all concept but a profoundly personal journey.

Looking beyond superficial markers of success is vital to finding true meaning and fulfillment. This shift in perspective enriches our lives and creates a ripple effect, inspiring and uplifting those around us.

Success, like beauty, is subjective—it exists in the eye of the beholder. Just as beauty is appreciated differently by each observer, success is defined by what each heart desires. This perspective encourages us to recognize and respect the unique and varied ways individuals find fulfillment and achieve their goals.

Success can often be measured by recognizing our impact on those around us—family, friends, colleagues, or the broader community. This happens when our actions make a positive difference in the lives of others. However, true success is not achieved overnight. It requires consistency, integrity, and a genuine commitment to living our values.

In today's fast-paced world, where personal gain often precedes everything else, many disregard anything that does not yield immediate benefits. However, lasting success is not just about accumulating wealth or status—it's about the legacy we leave behind. It's about how we contribute to humanity, make our families proud, and create a positive, lasting impact on society.

That is how I measure success.

An individual's mindset and demeanor deeply influence professional success. Knowledge, intellect, experience, and attitude all play crucial roles. Achieving professional success requires hard work, perseverance, patience, and professionalism, which can be measured through our daily business operations. However, professional success differs significantly from personal success, as one's professional mindset and attitude largely shape it.

But what truly matters in your pursuit of success? Is it financial achievements or the fulfillment that comes from accomplishing personal goals?

A motto I live by is: Financial Success ≠ Personal Fulfillment.

Financial success is evident everywhere—people have made and will continue making vast amounts of money. But does that necessarily mean they are all successful?

To answer that, we must first define what success means to us. What kind of success do our hearts desire? There are countless ways to make money. Some people build wealth through investments or gambling, but does that make them successful in a broader sense? Success, when combined with personal happiness and societal impact, takes on a completely different meaning.

Financial success is just one aspect of a larger picture. In many cases, it is not the defining measure of real success. When we look at individuals who have accumulated significant wealth, such as cricketers, movie stars, or business leaders, we often see that they begin searching for deeper meaning after reaching a certain level of financial achievement. Many turn to philanthropy, start NGOs, establish charitable foundations, or contribute to social causes.

Take Bill Gates, Warren Buffett, and Narayana Murthy as examples. We recognize them as successful not only because of the wealth they've built but because of how they have used their resources to give back to society. Their legacies are not solely about money but the positive change they have created. This is one way to view financial success—not just as personal gain but as a means to contribute to the greater good.

At the same time, some individuals are considered highly successful despite never amassing great wealth. One such example is Oseola McCarty. Born in 1908 in Hattiesburg, Mississippi, McCarty worked as a washerwoman for most of her life. She believed in the dignity of hard work and saved diligently, accumulating $280,000 over the years. When she retired at the age of 86, she chose to donate $150,000 of her savings to fund scholarships at the University of Southern Mississippi, helping underprivileged yet talented students pursue higher education.

Her generosity inspired many in her community to contribute, leaving behind a legacy far greater than money alone could measure.

If your success is purely financial, those who will remember and appreciate you will likely be your immediate family—those who inherit your wealth. However, if you take initiatives that contribute to the betterment of society, such as planting a thousand trees, improving education, or providing healthcare, you will be remembered for generations. Consider Mother Teresa, who built institutions and provided medical care to the world's most vulnerable populations. Her impact continues to inspire, long after her passing.

True success is about leaving a lasting imprint—not just in the form of wealth but through meaningful contributions that improve the lives of others.

Considering these perspectives, financial success is not as critical as it may seem. While financial stability is essential in many aspects of life, wealth alone is not the ultimate measure of success. In some cases, an exclusive focus on financial gain can even lead to destruction and unhappiness. I would never define success solely by someone's wealth or possessions, as financial achievements are not the be-all and end-all of a meaningful life.

Even those who have accumulated substantial wealth often turn to philanthropy, seeking to impact society positively. Their motivation goes beyond money—they desire to be remembered for something greater. A powerful example of this is the story behind the Nobel Prize.

As the story goes, Alfred Nobel found a newspaper obituary that mistakenly reported his death instead of his brother Ludvig's. The article referred to him as the "Merchant of Death," condemning him for his role in developing deadly explosives.

This profoundly saddened Nobel, making him realize that this was not the legacy he wanted to leave behind. Determined to be remembered for something more meaningful, he dedicated much of his fortune to establishing a foundation to recognize and reward contributions to humanity. This decision led to the creation of the Nobel Prize, demonstrating how true fulfillment comes from giving back to society rather than simply accumulating wealth.

As I address the younger generation, please reflect on what you want to be recognized for and remembered by when you reach a particular stage in life. Do you want to be known for exploiting natural resources or deceiving others for financial gain? Or do you want to be remembered as someone who positively impacted lives and contributed to the betterment of the world? The choice is yours. Leaving a meaningful legacy is a responsibility we all share.

Redefining Success Metrics

After completing my engineering degree, I entered the professional world with a clear goal—to support my family as the eldest of three siblings. With my younger brother and sister still in school, my father's financial burden fell on me, and I felt a deep responsibility to ease that load. Motivated by this, I began my career as a lecturer at the institution where I studied engineering. It gave me a sense of accomplishment, yet my aspirations continued to evolve.

My desire to pursue a master's degree soon altered my path. Determined to advance my knowledge while maintaining financial stability, I pursued my master's degree part-time while continuing to work as a lecturer.

After earning my master's, I was eager to enter the corporate world, innovate, and use my skills to increase my income.

However, life had other plans. A sudden tragedy struck when my father passed away, leaving me with the enormous responsibility of providing for my family. To ensure their well-being, I relocated, seeking a place where my family could find comfort and security.

This transition demanded immense dedication. I worked nearly 20 hours a day, juggling multiple assignments—teaching at a college while working in product development at various companies. The physical exhaustion and demanding routine were overwhelming, yet I remained steadfast. Every second of my time became an opportunity to push forward, driven by the responsibility to create a better future for my family.

In hindsight, while my hard work may have been perceived as a success, it was not sustainable. I had always dreamed of earning a degree from a prestigious institution like IISc/IIT, believing that attaining a higher level of knowledge would add value to my endeavors. Determined to push myself further, I pursued a PhD from the Indian Institute of Science (IISc). After clearing the necessary entrance exams and interviews, I secured a seat in one of IISc's top departments. Given my family responsibilities and a seven-year academic gap, I set an ambitious goal—to complete my PhD in three years. With unwavering focus, I completed my academic projects and submitted my thesis in three and a half years.

Upon earning my PhD, I transitioned from a frugally paid job with 18 to 20-hour workdays to a corporate position that doubled my salary. At the time, I considered this a significant success. However, as life progressed, my interpretation of success evolved. I soon sought a more impactful role within an organization—one where I could contribute meaningfully.

I achieved this at an offshore development center for a top multinational company, working in R&D and meeting critical work targets. My professional growth and increased salary further reinforced my idea of success.

At that stage, real success meant continuous learning and growth within my company or organization. But as I observed the business landscape, I noticed a recurring cycle—large corporations breaking down, smaller companies rising to prominence, and the entire corporate ecosystem undergoing constant restructuring. These shifts made me question whether working for a prestigious company, excelling in my role, and earning a lucrative salary were the ultimate measures of success. While such achievements are valid, they become irrelevant if the organization struggles or collapses.

This realization deeply troubled me and forced me to reflect on my purpose. I began thinking about sustainable success, which would remain meaningful regardless of external circumstances. At this juncture, I embarked on a social innovation journey, using my skills to address societal challenges. I left prestigious job titles and hefty paychecks to focus on something more fulfilling—serving my community.

At 50, I set out to make a tangible difference. I developed medical devices to facilitate early eye screenings, test kidney function, and enable healthcare professionals to diagnose remotely. These innovations have had a profound impact, helping people detect health issues early and prevent serious complications. The satisfaction that comes from making a societal impact is immeasurable. It's not about the money earned, but the lives touched and the difference made. I have had the privilege of positively impacting the lives of 8 to 10 million people globally—a source of immense pride. The recognition from my community, reflected in numerous awards and accolades, serves as a testament to the value of my efforts. But beyond the accolades, the real change I have witnessed in people's lives defines the true meaning of success for me.

Innovating for the Masses

As the study above corroborates, financial wealth alone is insufficient to achieve real success. Let me share my experience with innovating for the masses, particularly in the context of India's inadequate healthcare system. Unlike commodities such as petroleum or gold, healthcare costs continue to rise over time, rarely decreasing.

Our forefathers taught us that prevention is better than a cure. Yet, despite this wisdom, we often wait until symptoms appear before seeking treatment rather than prioritizing preventive care. The truth is that preventive measures could solve up to 80% of our health problems.

With this in mind, I focused on developing technologies, protocols, procedures, and clinical pathways centered around preventive care. While doctors are on the frontlines of healthcare, technologists play a crucial role in equipping them with innovative tools. We are responsible for improving healthcare outcomes by bridging the gap between medicine and technology.

A Personal Catalyst for Innovation

A personal experience that deeply motivated me to innovate in preventive and mobile healthcare was my father's untimely passing.

Coming from a humble background, my father worked as an accounts officer in a small camp at one of the gold mines in North Karnataka.

Despite being physically fit at the age of 53, he suffered a heart attack and was rushed to the local hospital. Tragically, the hospital only had a visiting cardiologist from the district hospital once a month. With no immediate medical intervention available, my father suffered a second, fatal heart attack.

This devastating loss underscored the urgent need for accessible, preventive healthcare solutions. I realized that timely diagnosis and early intervention could save countless lives. This realization fueled my commitment to developing innovative technologies to address health issues before they become life-threatening.

Bridging the Urban-Rural Healthcare Divide

When I moved to Bangalore, I was struck by the abundance of medical facilities in the city. However, I couldn't help but think about people in rural and remote areas—places like where my father had lived. I asked cardiologists about patients in such regions, and their response was often the same: it was the responsibility of the local cardiologist.

But what if there were no local cardiologists available? Why couldn't we leverage technology to bridge the gap? What if ECG data from remote locations could be sent to urban centers, where specialists could review and diagnose patients remotely?

I realized that we could make this possible by harnessing the three Cs of technology: Computation, Communication, and Collaboration.

• Computation would enable real-time analysis of ECG data.

• Communication would facilitate the secure transmission of medical data from rural areas to urban centers.

• Collaboration would ensure that specialists could provide timely diagnoses and medical advice regardless of location.

By integrating these three elements, we could prevent fatalities like my father's and countless others by overcoming the limitations of healthcare accessibility.

Overcoming Challenges in Healthcare Innovation

However, implementing such solutions in India came with significant challenges. The healthcare system was complex, and regulatory hurdles made the process even more difficult. I couldn't help but ask: Why were these solutions not being implemented in India, especially when they were already available in developed countries?

India does not lack intelligence or capability. I have firsthand experience in high-performance computing and AI, working with leading companies like Ericsson in the telecom industry. Inspired by the potential to make a real difference, I made a bold decision—I left my high-profile job at a multinational corporation to focus on making healthcare more affordable and accessible through technology-driven solutions.

The specific problem I set out to solve was the lack of affordable and accessible healthcare in rural areas, a gap that was leading to preventable illnesses and deaths. My mission became clear: to develop solutions to bridge this divide and ensure that quality healthcare was no longer a privilege confined to urban centers but a fundamental right accessible to all.

This decision led me to launch my business ventures, driven by a singular goal—using technology to bridge the gap in healthcare accessibility and affordability in India. My journey in healthcare began in the late 1990s when I worked with Ericsson in Stockholm, Sweden. Since then, I have been involved in various aspects of healthcare, from physical health to connectivity and its advantages for post-cardiac arrest patients.

Later, when I joined Philips as a technical director and manager, I became more deeply involved in medical technology and healthcare informatics. During this time, I realized a fundamental issue—most of our healthcare efforts focused on sick care rather than preventive care. While healthcare systems worldwide were advancing, the emphasis remained on treating illnesses rather than preventing them. I firmly believed that preventive care was the most effective solution, the most affordable, and sustainable form of healthcare.

In 2007, I saw this as an urgent need for India. Today, it is a necessity for the entire world. The old saying goes, "Prevention is better than a cure." Yet, making prevention a reality has always been easier said than done.

The Birth of Forus Health

With a clear vision and an unwavering desire to make a difference, I took a leap of faith. In 2010, I co-founded Forus Health Private Limited with a trusted friend who shared my passion for making healthcare more accessible and affordable through innovative technology.

The name Forus was carefully chosen—it symbolizes health and community, embodying our mission from the beginning. Our focus on ophthalmology was not just about developing medical devices but also championing preventive care and ensuring healthcare accessibility, particularly in rural areas. What began as a personal journey soon evolved into a mission to serve the masses.

A Defining Career Transition

Life is a series of moments that shape our destiny. In 1987 I made a critical transition when I relocated from Mysore to Bangalore. I was working as a lecturer at the time, but I wanted to shift from academia to the industry. I knocked on countless doors, attended interviews, and engaged with professionals in the field.

Finding a job in engineering colleges was easy, but industry professionals questioned my six-year teaching experience. They often emphasized how different academia was from industry, making me wonder if I was overlooked for opportunities. During this period of uncertainty and self-doubt, I began contemplating a different path—becoming a job provider instead of a job seeker.

This realization proved to be a turning point. Not long after, I had the opportunity to co-found a company. This experience broadened my perspective and strengthened my resolve to create and innovate rather than follow a predetermined career path.

Following this entrepreneurial experience, I pursued my PhD at IISc, a decision that would further shape my career trajectory. Once I submitted my thesis, finding jobs became significantly easier—perhaps due to the IISc brand or my growing reputation as an innovator with a strong drive to create something new. This shift in mindset allowed me to approach challenges differently, opening doors that had once seemed out of reach.

Taking the Entrepreneurial Leap

In 2010, I boldly decided to step away from corporate security and venture into entrepreneurship. It was not an easy path. We faced numerous challenges, from securing funding to building the right team.

However, we remained unwavering in our mission—to identify pressing societal problems and develop innovative solutions that would lead to a healthier society.

Despite the well-known adage, "Prevention is better than cure," practical action in healthcare was still lacking. Around 2007-2008, most healthcare efforts focused on sick care, with people seeking medical attention only after falling ill. However, the rise of lifestyle diseases like diabetes, hypertension, and cardiovascular conditions demonstrated that early detection and prevention were the only sustainable solutions.

One of the pivotal moments in my journey was my visit to Aravind Eye Hospital in Madurai. I had the privilege of interacting with the founder, Dr. Venkataswamy. His inspiring story and unwavering commitment to making quality eye care accessible to all deeply resonated with me. His passion reinforced my belief that technology could—and should—be leveraged to bring healthcare to those who needed it the most.

This experience motivated me to partner with my colleague, Mr. Chandrasekhar, to establish Forus Health. Our mission was simple but ambitious—to make eye disease, early detection and prevention practical and realizable for millions.

These defining moments helped me redefine success. True success, I realized, is not just about personal achievements or financial gain—it is about using our knowledge, skills, and resources to create meaningful change that improves lives.

The Evolving Definition of Success

Success has always been an evolving concept for me, shifting like a drifting star or a moving goalpost. The vision of success in our youth can change drastically over time—what once seemed like the pinnacle of achievement at 20 may look entirely different at 30, 50, or beyond. Many people only begin redefining success after retiring from their regular careers at 60.

At one point, success meant excelling in exams, achieving distinctions, and securing admission to a prestigious college. But once I reached that milestone, I asked: What next? Over time, my definition of success evolved from personal achievements to making a meaningful impact. My experiences profoundly influenced this shift in perspective in the healthcare and wellness sector, where I saw firsthand the life-changing effects of early detection and prevention.

A Childhood Fueled by Curiosity

As a child, electronics fascinated me, and I was determined to pursue a career in the field. When computers emerged, I naturally gravitated toward hardware engineering, leading me to study electronics and computer hardware. However, growing up in a remote gold mine camp, educational resources were limited. Learning was challenging without internet and a few books, but I was determined to overcome these obstacles.

I borrowed books from my cousins in Bangalore, seizing every opportunity to expand my knowledge. These early experiences shaped my passion for learning and problem-solving, instilling a deep commitment to overcoming challenges—an attitude that would later define my professional and entrepreneurial journey.

A Passion for Electronics and Perseverance in Education

One incident stands out vividly from my early years. I came across notes from my cousin detailing how to build a transistor radio. Without a photocopier, I meticulously copied everything onto plain sheets by hand. My enthusiasm for electronics fueled this endeavor, and I immersed myself in every detail.

During my 11th and 12th standard, I worked relentlessly to secure a spot on the merit list, ensuring admission to a top engineering college in Bangalore or Mysore. Fortunately, my hard work paid off—I scored well in my exams and was admitted to one of the best engineering colleges in Mysore. At the time, this achievement felt like the most tremendous success of my life.

Reaching that milestone brought me immense satisfaction, but the initial excitement soon gave way to the pressure of proving myself. Success was no longer just about getting into a good college—it became about excelling academically, achieving high grades, and securing a promising job. Success, I realized, is not a single event but a continuous journey, unfolding incrementally.

Electronics and computer hardware drove that journey for me. My aspirations went beyond securing a job; I wanted to push the boundaries of innovation, make meaningful contributions to my field, and ultimately impact people's lives.

Balancing Higher Studies and Innovation

After completing my engineering degree, I pursued a part-time master's degree while working—a common path for many. However, I was determined to set myself apart.

Instead of following a conventional trajectory, I sought unique opportunities that would allow me to apply my knowledge practically.

I explored industries such as textile and rubber, envisioning how automation and technology could enhance efficiency and revolutionize these sectors. Fortunately, my college encouraged such initiatives, allowing me to balance my role as a lecturer with hands-on consulting work.

This experience brought me deep satisfaction, not just as an engineer but as an innovator. It reinforced my belief that success is not merely about what you achieve but how you apply your knowledge to create real-world impact.

In 1988-89, driven by my passion for innovation in electronics and computers, I embarked on an entrepreneurial journey with two friends—Santosh, a marketing expert, and Harsha, a skilled software developer. Together, we founded Knoxware, a company dedicated to developing the Knox card, an antivirus solution designed to combat emerging computer viruses.

This was another milestone in my journey—a success in business and creating something that served a societal need. The fulfillment of building an innovative solution that addressed a real problem reinforced my belief in the power of technology to create a meaningful impact.

A Lifelong Commitment to Innovation and Learning

My journey in innovation has been a continuous learning process, pushing me to seek new opportunities and solutions. Immersing myself in society's challenges helped me identify real problems, empathize with those affected, and develop innovative solutions.

My tenure at Ericsson R&D was a masterclass in product marketing and quality maintenance.

My role at Philips as an innovation manager and technical director deepened my understanding of patenting, hidden innovations, knowledge management, and incremental and disruptive innovations.

These experiences made me question whether I could share this knowledge with others. Could I use my expertise to build something that would impact society more?

This realization shifted my definition of success. I left my corporate roles to start my own company, where I could innovate, create products, sell them globally, and make meaningful contributions to society. However, as success evolved, so did the challenges that came with it.

Challenges on the Road to Success

Success is never an individual achievement—it involves teams, communities, and society. Multiple external factors influence success, often presenting hurdles that must be overcome.

1. The Challenge of Financial Support

One of the most significant barriers to success is financial backing. For those with financial security, the journey becomes significantly easier. However, not everyone has that privilege. Entrepreneurs like me have had to carefully balance finances, sustainability, and societal impact, ensuring that financial constraints do not limit innovation.

2. The Challenge of Gaining Support from Others

Your efforts often go unrecognized until you achieve something substantial, even by those closest to you. While I may be personally motivated, keeping my family and team motivated was a different challenge.

The key was communication—helping them understand why my work mattered, how it contributed to the greater good, and why it would ultimately lead to a better future for everyone involved. Every individual has confidence in their passions, but their family or peers do not always share that confidence. Clear and consistent communication is essential to eliminating misunderstandings and aligning everyone with the vision.

3. The Challenge of the Right Environment

The ecosystem plays a crucial role in nurturing success. I recall an instance when a company approached me with a groundbreaking propulsion system that could reduce rocket fuel consumption by 100 times. However, despite the promising technology, we faced a significant challenge: testing.

Unlike ISRO, which had well-established laboratory setups, this company wanted to conduct tests privately. The issue wasn't the technology but the lack of an environment conducive to such innovation. Even the most revolutionary ideas struggle to take off without supporting infrastructure, regulatory frameworks, and industry collaboration.

4. The Challenge of Mindset and Adoption

An environment for innovation and growth is impossible without a mindset that embraces new ideas. A country or society's adoption rate of new technology often depends on its openness to change.

• Some nations rapidly integrate emerging technologies, fostering economic and societal growth.

• Others hesitate, weighed down by conservatism, skepticism, and rigid mindsets.

For true innovation to thrive, we must pursue new initiatives and foster a culture that encourages bold solutions. Societal progress is not just about technological advancements but also about changing how people think, adapt, and embrace the future.

Overcoming the Hurdles to Success

These challenges—financial limitations, lack of recognition, ecosystem constraints, and mindset barriers—are just some of the obstacles to success. However, true innovation is about navigating these challenges, finding solutions, and continuously pushing forward.

Success is not about avoiding obstacles but overcoming them, adapting to the landscape, and leaving a lasting impact.

Success can be achieved in many ways, as no singular formula guarantees it for everyone. In the next section, we will explore unconventional paths to success.

One of the most influential figures in my life was my father. A commerce graduate, he began his career in social education, where he made a meaningful impact as a social inspector. He guided and supported young individuals with academic potential, ensuring they received the education and mentorship they needed to build a better future.

Later, he moved to a small camp in the gold mines, home to about 400 families. He joined as an accountant and later became a supervisor and an accounts officer. However, regardless of his position, he always exceeded his official responsibilities.

While others completed their shifts and returned home to their families, my father spent evenings helping others. There was a society store and canteen in the camp, and after work, he would voluntarily assist with bookkeeping and financial management, ensuring that records were maintained correctly. He firmly believed in using his qualifications, skills, and experience to help small establishments that lacked professional financial expertise.

His commitment to community service extended beyond work. He initiated a dairy project with some friends, managing operations and ensuring its success. Additionally, he played a key role in establishing a trust to foster unity among people of different religious and social backgrounds. As part of this initiative, the community would gather weekly for satsangs or bhajans, creating a shared spiritual and social connection space.

My father was always passionate about bringing people together through spirituality, cooperative farming, or community initiatives. Growing up, I didn't fully grasp the significance of his actions, but today, I sincerely appreciate the values he instilled in me. His selfless dedication to uplifting others has profoundly shaped my perspective on success and contribution.

Another individual who has greatly influenced me is Dr. R.A. Mashelkar. I was honored to receive his first Inclusive Innovation Award, which he established in his mother's name—the Anjali Mashelkar Inclusive Innovation Award.

Before meeting him, I had only read about his remarkable contributions, particularly his work in patents and intellectual property rights in India. Dr. Mashelkar was instrumental in challenging and preventing the patenting of natural Indian resources such as turmeric and rice, when there was a global push to patent traditional knowledge and indigenous products. As Director General of CSIR (Council of Scientific & Industrial Research), his work profoundly impacted India's scientific and innovation landscape.

Meeting him was an eye-opening experience. His journey from humble beginnings to becoming the Director General of one of India's most prestigious research institutions deeply inspired me. His story reinforced my belief that success comes from perseverance, vision, and a commitment to societal progress.

Dr. Mashelkar is one of my greatest inspirations and my guru. I strive to integrate his philosophy of "getting more from less for more"—maximizing resources to create a greater impact for a more significant number of people—into my work.

Throughout my career, I have had the privilege of working with and learning from many inspiring individuals. One such inspiration is George Smith.

George came to India to establish Motorola's R&D center in Bangalore. Unlike many expats in similar roles, he was committed to building the center entirely with local talent. While others might have hired professionals from abroad, George believed India had sufficient homegrown expertise. He recruited skilled individuals from institutions like the Indian Institute of Science (IISc), IITs, and regional engineering colleges, ensuring that the center maintained global standards while fostering local innovation.

I had the privilege of working closely with him during this time and witnessed his innovative approach, dedication, and leadership firsthand. Within three to four years, he successfully built Motorola's software development center in India, taking it to SEI CMM Level 5—the highest level of software process maturity.

However, George wasn't content with just corporate success. After achieving this milestone, he wanted to apply his knowledge to create a more significant societal impact. Taking a bold step, he founded CG Smith Software, not to develop another software product, but to teach scalable building and training processes. His vision was to help other companies achieve CMM Level 5 through structured tools and training, ensuring long-term excellence in software development.

During my two and a half years of working with him, I gained invaluable insights that continue to shape my professional journey. His ability to merge technical expertise with a mission-driven approach was truly inspiring, and I have always cherished the knowledge I gained during that time. I have made it my mission to nurture and share this knowledge with others, ensuring that his legacy of innovation and mentorship continues.

My father, George Smith, and Dr. R.A. Mashelkar's success stories were not about accumulating wealth or material possessions. Instead, they were about giving back to society, making meaningful contributions, and inspiring future generations. These individuals laid the foundation for purpose-driven success, showing how people like us can lead with impact and innovation.

Their actions and philosophies have profoundly influenced my business and personal development approach. I have learned that success is measured by financial gains and the ability to create positive change. Their dedication to mentorship, innovation, and societal progress continues to guide my professional journey. While financial sustainability is essential in any business, deep tech and high-impact industries, such as healthcare, require a broader definition of success. Traditional companies measure performance through top-line and bottom-line growth, assessing revenues and profits on a quarterly, monthly, or annual basis.

However, success cannot be solely defined by financial metrics in industries that shape lives and drive long-term innovation. In healthcare, technology, and social impact, we must also consider how our work contributes to human well-being, accessibility, and sustainable progress.

As professionals in business, innovation, and personal development, our roles extend beyond financial success. Our contributions to society, technological advancements, and meaningful change are equally, if not more, valuable. It is this holistic approach to success that truly defines our legacy.

A structured system is essential for measuring success beyond financial metrics. Professor Kandachar from Delft University proposed one such solution in his thesis, introducing the triple bottom line concept.

The triple bottom line is a framework that suggests businesses should focus on three key performance areas: financial, social, and environmental impact.

• Financial success is the first metric, evaluating a company's revenue and profitability.

• Social impact is the second, measuring how many lives are touched and improved by a company's product or service.

• Environmental responsibility is the third, assessing how eco-friendly and sustainable a business's approach is. This includes green initiatives, energy and water conservation, and sustainable financial practices contributing to a healthier ecosystem.

For a company to claim success, it must achieve all three bottom lines. This holistic approach ensures that next-generation businesses focus on financial growth and societal and environmental contributions. It is an excellent model for measuring impact, and I implement it across all my ventures to ensure they meet these three parameters. Professor Kandachar's framework has been widely appreciated, and many companies are now integrating the triple bottom line into their core narratives and operational strategies.

Creating a new enterprise, generating revenue, and doing good for society is rewarding. However, it is equally important to redefine what success truly means. Companies like Tesla and Patagonia have achieved financial success and significant societal and environmental contributions.

Design thinking is essential to driving social innovation. It means stepping out of your comfort zone and developing solutions that address fundamental societal challenges. True innovation requires immersion in the problem, understanding it at its core, and designing solutions that help people overcome difficulties.

This approach is rooted in empathy—the ability to understand the needs of end users and create solutions tailored to them. Empathy is not just a buzzword but a fundamental principle of design thinking, driving innovation and meaningful societal impact.

Revenue generation is evolving in today's world. Everyone wants to start a startup, but it is not just about building a business, but about developing solutions that address societal issues.

Successful innovation requires frugality—getting more from less. This mindset is crucial for the next generation of entrepreneurs, particularly in a country like India, where affordable solutions in education and healthcare are in high demand. These sectors present enormous opportunities for innovation and transformation, offering significant rewards for those who can develop effective and scalable solutions.

This will be the mantra for the next generation: impact-driven, frugal innovation that creates value beyond financial gains.

Through my professional ventures, I have achieved success by positively influencing society, and in return, I have been honored with recognition and acclaim. This brings us to the next point.

There have been several occasions where people have appreciated our work. For example, when I worked for corporations, few people outside my close relatives knew what I did. At social gatherings or functions, people would greet me politely, ask how my work was going, or inquire about which country I had visited, and we would engage in casual conversation. However, once I began developing innovations and creating products that impacted society, people's perception of me changed.

They started looking up to me, encouraging their children to learn from my experiences and seek my advice about their careers, education, or courses to pursue. This shift in recognition was not because of titles or corporate roles, but because my work had tangible, visible effects on people's lives.

Another form of recognition has come through the awards and accolades we have received from various academic councils, engineering institutions, and medical colleges. Attending major conferences has also given us tremendous appreciation for our contributions.

Society is actively seeking newer, better, and more impactful innovations, particularly in healthcare and education, that are inclusive and capable of transforming lives at scale. The encouragement and acknowledgment we receive reinforce our mission to continue innovating in ways that create real-world impact.

While I sincerely appreciate the recognition and status that come with our work, I strive to remain humble and grounded by continuing to engage in grassroots-level projects. These projects provide endless learning opportunities, offering invaluable insights that fuel my drive for innovation.

The personal satisfaction and fulfillment I derive from these initiatives are unparalleled. Translating what I have learned into new solutions or products would be my greatest success—something I continuously aspire to achieve.

Although I have accomplished several milestones, there is still a long way to go. The journey of societal impact and innovation is not just about the final results but also about the personal growth, learning, and fulfillment that come along the way.

We must move beyond the idea that success is defined solely by money and material possessions. Instead, we should measure success by the meaningful impact we create and the positive outcomes that benefit society.

The accurate benchmark of success should be a tangible, positive change in our communities, whether through education, healthcare, or technological advancements. Fostering efficient teamwork and building a collaborative ecosystem can enhance success and propel innovation to greater heights.

2

THE POWER OF
TEAMWORK

*"The strength of the team is each individual member. The strength of
each member is the team."*

— Phil Jackson

H ave you ever marveled at the beauty of a symphony, where each
musician plays in perfect harmony to produce a collective
masterpiece? With a mere gesture, the conductor unites various
instruments—strings, brass, woodwinds, and percussion—each
contributing its unique sound to create something larger than itself.

The violin's delicate melody intertwines with the cello's deep
resonance, while the trumpet's bold voice adds triumph and energy.
Percussion keeps the rhythm steady, driving the piece forward.
No single instrument dominates; instead, the synchronization and
blending of individual talents create something far greater than the
sum of its parts.

The magic of a symphony lies not only in the technical skill of each
musician but also in their ability to listen, respond, and collaborate.

Each note, each breath, and each stroke of the bow contributes to the collective sound—a sound that would be incomplete without the entire orchestra working in unity. It is a delicate balance, a shared goal, and an interdependence that make the performance extraordinary.

This interdependence is mirrored in business, where every team member drives success. Just as in an orchestra, a business thrives on collaboration, synchronization, and the collective strength of its people.

Now, imagine the potential of this harmony in business and entrepreneurship.

Throughout my career, I have worked with remarkable individuals who have profoundly shaped my personal and professional growth. These collaborators and mentors provided more than opportunities—they fundamentally influenced how I approached challenges, leadership, and innovation.

Reflecting on the key figures who have impacted my journey, I realize their lessons were pivotal in guiding my career path.

One of the most influential leaders I worked with was the CEO of Philips India during my tenure at Philips Innovation Campus. He had an extraordinary ability to simplify even the most complex problems—a trait that deeply resonated with me and ultimately shaped my leadership style.

Another defining moment in my career was my transition from project manager to innovation manager. This shift taught me the art of motivating and inspiring teams across various roles without directly managing them. It was a crucial lesson in influence, leadership, and strategic thinking.

These experiences—and the environments these leaders created—helped cultivate the skills, insights, and leadership approach that define my work today.

When I joined Philips, I had the opportunity to work closely with the CEO of Philips India—an experience that left an indelible mark on my career.

My boss had an uncanny ability to break down complex issues and make them seem simple. He could distill problems to their core, often infusing humor into the process, and then offer a solution that, in retrospect, felt almost obvious. His approach was finding answers and making the process approachable, collaborative, and engaging.

One of my earliest and most memorable interactions with the CEO occurred during my interview at Philips Innovation Campus. At the time, I assumed the campus was bustling with innovation managers—a vibrant hub of like-minded individuals working on groundbreaking projects.

Eager to understand the scope of my role, I asked, "How many innovation managers are already working here?"

His answer surprised me.

"None. That's why we're looking for you."

That response wasn't just a recruitment statement—it was a lesson in leadership, trust, and the value of initiative. It taught me that opportunities for innovation often arise in spaces where structure is still being built, and that being the first in a role is not a limitation but an open canvas for creativity and impact.

The name "Philips Innovation Campus" suggested I was stepping into a space teeming with innovation. However, during my conversation with the Chief, he explained that the center was initially called the "Philips Software Center." He had renamed it to reflect the company's broader aspirations—it was no longer just about software; he envisioned a hub that embraced all forms of innovation.

This was more than just a name change—it was a profound shift in mindset, and I was tasked with helping to bring that vision to life.

This conversation taught me two key lessons:

Innovation often begins with how we frame things. Simply renaming the center created a new space for innovation to thrive, shifting how people perceived and approached their work.

The power of a blank canvas. The Chief trusted me to build something from the ground up, giving me the freedom to shape the future of the innovation center. It was both a challenge and an immense opportunity.

In today's fast-paced, globalized, and interconnected world, individual brilliance can shine, but the collective power of a team drives the most impactful and lasting successes.

Like in a symphony, where musicians collaborate to create a unified masterpiece, businesses thrive when team members align their strengths and build on one another's expertise. The complexity of modern challenges—from navigating market shifts to competing in high-stakes industries—demands individual excellence and collective synergy.

The era of the "lone genius" carrying an entire organization on their shoulders is long gone. While iconic leaders like Steve Jobs and Elon

Musk are often portrayed as singular visionaries, the reality behind their success is far more nuanced. Behind every visionary is a team of engineers, designers, marketers, and strategists, each playing their role in bringing an idea to life.

Innovation rarely happens in isolation. It results from collaborative brainstorming, merging different perspectives, and integrating varied skill sets.

Today's business challenges are too complex for anyone to tackle alone. Whether it's:

• Developing cutting-edge technology

• Expanding into new markets

• Navigating regulatory landscapes

Companies need teams with diverse expertise to approach problems from multiple angles, drive innovation, and execute strategies effectively. Just as a symphony relies on different instruments to create its rich, layered sound, businesses thrive on collaborating with varied skill sets.

This necessity of teamwork should reassure you of the value of your collaborative efforts and instill confidence in your team's ability to overcome challenges.

A popular saying perfectly captures this idea:

"If you want to go fast, go alone. If you want to go far, go together."

This proverb resonates deeply with me. I have experienced both—the speed of working alone and the limitations of isolation.

In the early stages of my career, particularly when we founded Knoxware, I relished the independence of working alone.

The project was small and straightforward—a proof of concept that I had envisioned from start to finish. Because I understood the project entirely, I could work efficiently without explaining my ideas or aligning with others. In just a few days, I had turned my vision into reality.

That initial phase of working solo was exhilarating. I had complete control, the freedom to make quick decisions, and the ability to move at my own pace, seeing immediate progress. Without the responsibilities of managing a team, I could focus entirely on execution.

However, as I soon discovered, this speed came with limitations.

Advantages of Working Individually	Disadvantages of Working Individually
Be the boss	Long time
Take Full Credit	No Help
Easy to focus	Sole Responsibility
Decide what to do and when	No one to motivate
Become Independent	Constraints in Ideas
No outside pressure	If delayed
They are fast	Not many skills
No need to distribute the work	Too much stress
Know what is going on	It can be a bit boring
More clarity	
A challenge to work alone	

While I quickly developed the proof of concept, transitioning from concept to a fully functional product required much more than individual effort. The following steps in Knoxware's journey—refining the user interface, marketing the product, and managing customer service—were beyond what I could handle alone. To make the product market-ready, I needed a team with specialized skills, particularly software development expertise.

At this point, the limitations of working alone became evident. No matter how skilled or efficient I was, the project's complexity demanded a broader range of expertise. It became clear that a team was essential, not just for sharing the workload but also for bringing new perspectives and ideas. Without collaboration, the product could never reach its full potential, and my ability to innovate would be constrained by the limitations of working in isolation.

Fortunately, my co-founder stepped in to help recruit and build a team, enabling us to move forward. With the right team, we could delegate tasks, collaborate on ideas, and collectively take the product to market. This experience reinforced an important lesson:

Even the most brilliant ideas need the support of others to materialize fully.

Work is more than just completing tasks; it builds connections and fosters relationships. One of the biggest challenges of working alone is the lack of human interaction that naturally comes with teamwork.

When we collaborate, we're not just sharing the workload—we're sharing experiences, learning from one another, and supporting each other through challenges. These connections make work more enjoyable and fulfilling.

There is undoubtedly a place for individual work, especially in the early stages of a project, when ideas are still taking shape. Sometimes, working alone allows for greater focus and creativity. However, as I've learned from experience, the key to success is finding the right balance between independence and collaboration.

Later in my career, while leading the Research and Development (R&D) division at Ericsson in India, I encountered another striking example of the limitations of working alone. This time, it wasn't my experience, but that of a highly skilled engineer who had relocated to India from one of Ericsson's international offices.

This individual was exceptionally talented, and his assignment required him to work independently on a specific project. At first, it seemed like an ideal setup—he had the experience, knowledge, and autonomy to manage the project independently. My role was to provide him with the necessary infrastructure and resources, and in many ways, he thrived in this environment.

However, over time, it became clear that working in isolation had significant professional and personal drawbacks.

As the sole person assigned to the project, he often worked late into the night, fully immersed in his task. However, on other days, I would notice him wandering around the office, grabbing coffee, and engaging in casual conversations without urgency.

His productivity fluctuated noticeably, correlating with the absence of a team around him. Even though he was friendly and well-liked by his colleagues, the nature of his work meant that he often felt isolated.

• There was no one to share ideas with

• No team to brainstorm solutions

• No sense of camaraderie to keep him motivated during challenging times

This isolation affected not only his productivity but also his overall job satisfaction. Despite his competence, it became evident that the absence of teamwork left him detached and unsupported.

This experience reinforced another critical lesson: Even the most talented individuals need a team, not just for collaboration but also for motivation, accountability, and long-term success.

The engineer's experience at Ericsson was a powerful reminder of the importance of collaboration. Even though he had all the skills and resources needed to succeed, the isolation he experienced took a toll on his well-being. He was an incredibly talented individual, but working in solitude limited his potential to grow and thrive within the organization.

It became evident that while solo work might offer short-term advantages, it cannot replace the long-term benefits of teamwork.

The Importance of Teamwork in Work and Life

Work is like a game—just like any game, it's much more enjoyable when played with a team. Working alongside others creates a sense of shared purpose and accomplishment, offering opportunities for learning and growth that are impossible when working alone.

Companies must balance individual work and teamwork with the increasing need for remote and hybrid work environments. In India, we have learned from multinational companies that effectively use modern collaborative tools for project management, such as GitHub, Trello, and UltiMatix. Thanks to the COVID-19 pandemic, these tools have become widely accepted and integrated into workplaces worldwide.

To maintain an effective balance between individual work and teamwork, key strategies include:

• Setting clear goals at both the individual and team levels

• Using open communication tools like WhatsApp and Slack

• Understanding personal strengths and weaknesses

• Actively supporting team members

• Ensuring that individual goals align with the overall team objectives

This approach allows individuals to contribute their unique skills while working effectively toward shared goals.

Key Points to Consider for Effective Teamwork

• **Self-awareness:** Know your strengths and areas where you excel individually, and understand how these strengths can best benefit the team.

• **Clear goal setting:** Define SMART goals (Specific, Measurable, Achievable, Relevant, and Time-bound) for individual and team performance.

• **Open communication:** Regularly share updates, feedback, and concerns with your team to maintain transparency and alignment.

• **Role definition:** Understand your assigned role within the team and how your contributions fit the bigger picture.

• **Active listening:** Focus on your teammates' needs and perspectives to foster collaboration.

• **Collaboration skills:** Be willing to share ideas, provide constructive feedback, and actively participate in discussions.

• **Conflict resolution:** Address disagreements constructively and seek solutions that benefit the team.

• **Flexibility:** Be adaptable to changing situations and willing to adjust your approach based on team needs.

• **Celebrate successes:** Recognize and appreciate individual and team achievements to boost morale and motivation.

How to Apply These Strategies

• **During project planning:** Discuss individual responsibilities while ensuring they align with team goals.

• **Regular team meetings:** Use these sessions to share progress updates, address challenges, and discuss collaborative solutions.

• **Performance reviews:** Evaluate individual contributions while considering their impact on the team's success.

• **Seek feedback:** Ask for constructive feedback from team members to identify areas for improvement.

The Power of Teamwork in Achieving Greater Impact

Working alone can provide the clarity and speed needed to develop initial ideas, but teamwork transforms those ideas into something more significant and impactful.

Without collaboration, the scope of what we can achieve is limited, both by our abilities and the isolation of working alone.

By embracing teamwork, communication, and collaboration, we expand possibilities, accelerate innovation, and build stronger, more successful organizations.

The Power of Effective Teamwork

Throughout my career, I have worked on numerous projects, but one particular endeavor stands out as a pivotal moment where effective teamwork played a crucial role in the project's success. Unlike anything I had previously encountered, this project involved transferring technology from a U.S. company to India.

It required technical expertise, strong team coordination, clear communication, and effective leadership. Ultimately, the project's success was a testament to the power of teamwork, well-implemented processes, and the correct use of tools.

A Challenging Transition from Research to Industry

After researching at the Indian Institute of Science, I transitioned back into the industry, joining a small company specializing in software engineering. This company was tasked with an ambitious project: receiving technology transfer from Harris Communication, a U.S.-based firm in North Carolina, and adapting the solution for a different platform.

Beyond porting the solution, our objective was to manage the entire product lifecycle from India—a significant shift that required precision, adaptability, and strong execution.

Leading the Project: A Unique Set of Challenges

As the project manager, I was responsible for overseeing the entire project lifecycle, which included:

• Recruiting a capable team

• Collaborating closely with U.S. counterparts to understand the technology transfer

• Managing adaptation and implementation within a tight deadline

Given the complexity of the task, I knew from the outset that success would require more than individual effort—it demanded a strategic approach that considered multiple factors:

• Building the right team

• Equipping them with the appropriate tools

• Fostering a motivated and engaged workforce

By aligning these elements, organizations can create an environment where tasks are executed excellently, laying the foundation for long-term growth and success.

Overcoming Initial Skepticism

When the project was first given to us, the target seemed daunting. We were expected to complete the technology transfer and make necessary adaptations within three months—an incredibly tight timeline given the complexity of the task.

DR. SHYAM VASUDEVA RAO

I was initially skeptical about our ability to deliver on time. The project was filled with uncertainties, and the pressure to meet deadlines added to the challenge.

However, my skepticism faded as I assessed the company's resources and expertise. The organization had a strong reputation in software engineering, particularly in software quality and project management.

Their foundation in these areas became a game-changer, providing us with the support we needed to tackle challenges head-on.

Building the Right Team

Building the right team was one of the most critical steps in ensuring the project's success. As part of my role, I recruited 32 professionals within a month—a significant undertaking that required a clear and focused hiring strategy.

The key to effective teamwork, especially in a technically demanding project, is assembling a team with complementary skills. I deliberately selected team members with expertise in:

• Software engineering

• Project management

• Quality control

With the right people in place, we hit the ground running, ready to execute the project with precision and efficiency.

Here is how one can build a cohesive team:

1. Recruitment: Setting the Stage for Success

The foundation of any successful team is laid during the recruitment process. Assembling the right group of individuals requires more than just assessing technical skills—it necessitates a thorough understanding of interpersonal dynamics and cultural fit.

I advocate for involving team members in the recruitment process to ensure this.

When a team needs to hire a new member, the group lead should conduct the initial interviews, not HR alone. This approach ensures the recruitment leader is familiar with the team's needs and culture. Involving existing team members in the selection process allows them to evaluate how well potential candidates fit within the group dynamic.

This strategy fosters a sense of ownership and responsibility among team members, encouraging them to actively support the new hire's integration actively.

Additionally, setting clear expectations during the hiring phase is crucial. When the team is involved in selecting a new member, they gain a shared understanding of the required qualities and skills. This alignment ensures that everyone actively contributes to the new hire's success, laying the groundwork for collaboration before they even join the team.

2. Cultivating a Collaborative Mindset

A successful team thrives on a collaborative mindset that values mutual respect, support, and open communication.

To instill this mindset, I emphasize team-building activities, both formal and informal. Regular team outings, such as cricket matches or other sports events, help foster camaraderie and allow team members to bond outside the office environment.

These informal settings encourage individuals to interact freely, breaking down barriers that may exist within a structured work environment. By engaging in these shared experiences, teams develop stronger interpersonal relationships, improving their ability to communicate and collaborate effectively when faced with work-related challenges.

For example, participating in team-based obstacle courses or collaborative challenges reinforces shared purpose and mutual reliance, fostering trust and teamwork.

3. Clear Communication and Project Awareness

Communication is the lifeblood of any successful team. Every team member must know project objectives and their roles from the outset.

During project kick-off meetings, I ensure that every team member:

• Understands the project goals

• Knows their responsibilities

• Sees how their contributions fit into the larger picture

This clarity promotes accountability and empowers individuals to take ownership of their roles. When every team member understands the bigger picture, they are more engaged, motivated, and aligned toward collective success.

4. Celebrating Success: Recognition and Rewards

A strong team is built on motivation and recognition. Celebrating big and small successes is essential for maintaining morale and reinforcing the collaborative spirit.

After completing a project, I ensure we take the time to acknowledge every team member's hard work and dedication. This can be done through:

• Formal recognition programs

• Casual celebrations where team members share experiences and express gratitude

• Public acknowledgment of achievements

Implementing a structured rewards and recognition mechanism is crucial in this regard. Recognizing outstanding performances—whether through awards, promotions, public praise, or small tokens of appreciation—reinforces the value of collaboration.

This sends a clear message: "Individual contributions are valued, and success is a collective achievement."

Cultivating a positive team environment motivates members to collaborate, support one another, and strive for excellence.

5. Continuous Development and Learning

Building a cohesive team is an ongoing process that requires continuous development and learning. As industries evolve, so do the skills and knowledge required for success. Therefore, investing in the professional growth of team members is essential.

This can be achieved through:

• Workshops and training programs

• Mentorship opportunities

• Skill enhancement initiatives

Encouraging team members to share their expertise fosters a learning culture within the organization. When individuals feel empowered to contribute their insights, it enhances the collective skill set and strengthens relationships among team members.

Creating an environment where learning is valued and shared leads to greater collaboration and synergy, making team members feel more connected and engaged.

6. Fostering a Culture of Trust

Trust is the cornerstone of effective teamwork. To cultivate trust within the team, I emphasize:

• **Open communication** – encouraging team members to express ideas, concerns, and feedback in a safe environment.

• **Psychological safety** – ensuring individuals feel comfortable sharing their thoughts without fear of judgment.

• **Constructive discussions** – creating a space where innovative ideas can emerge and be refined.

A key factor in building trust is leading by example. As a leader, I strive to demonstrate:

- **Transparency** – being open about decisions and goals

- **Honesty** – fostering genuine and candid conversations

- **Reliability** – following through on commitments and being accountable

When team members see their leader as approachable and invested in their well-being, they feel encouraged to extend the same level of trust to one another. This culture of trust forms the foundation for collaboration, enabling teams to work together effectively toward shared goals.

A Team Fueled by Enthusiasm and a Shared Vision

From the moment the team was formed, there was a palpable sense of excitement. Everyone was eager to contribute, and there was a shared belief in the project's success.

Although this was a newly formed team, the fresh start created a positive environment where everyone felt motivated to give their best.

The Role of Tools and Processes

The success of this project wasn't dependent on any single individual. It was the result of:

- Collaboration

- A shared vision

- Effective teamwork

Every team member played a crucial role, and we achieved something remarkable together.

While the team's expertise was exceptional, our process-oriented approach set this project apart. The company had a robust set of software engineering tools, which we leveraged to manage project complexities efficiently. These tools helped us with:

• Tracking software requirements

• Managing projects efficiently

• Enhancing team communication

Here are some essential tools that enable teams to work cohesively, even across different time zones, ensuring that all aspects of the project are handled seamlessly from inception to delivery.

1. Unified Modeling Language (UML): Structuring Collaboration

One of the most fundamental tools for enhancing collaboration in software projects is the Unified Modeling Language (UML). UML plays a critical role in software development's planning and design stages by providing a standardized way to visualize system architecture and design.

At its core, UML helps teams:

• Create visual representations of software systems

• Map object models, data flows, and system behaviors

• Develop a shared language for developers, business analysts, and stakeholders

Using UML, teams can ensure everyone is on the same page regarding system design and functionality. This alignment makes it easier to:

• Gather requirements

• Structure system interactions

• Identify dependencies

UML helps break down complex systems into manageable components during the planning phase. It allows teams to:

• Visualize relationships between different system parts

• Define interactions between components

• Improve collaboration in distributed teams

Having a common design language is crucial for remote and distributed teams. By establishing clarity early in the project, teams can work more effectively, even when remotely operating.

2. Rational Suite: End-to-End Collaboration Tools

Alongside UML, one of the most critical toolsets I've used is the Rational Suite of products. Initially developed by Rational Software and now part of IBM's offering, these tools provide a comprehensive solution for managing software projects, from requirement gathering and design to testing and deployment.

The Rational Suite includes several powerful tools, such as:

• Rational Rose – Supports UML modeling

• ClearCase – A version control system for managing code development

These tools are invaluable for ensuring seamless collaboration throughout a project's lifecycle.

For instance, Rational Rose enables teams to automatically generate documentation using UML diagrams created during the design phase. This feature, known as Software Documentation Automation (SODA), ensures that all documentation is current without requiring manual intervention. This is particularly crucial in large teams or client-facing projects, where accurate documentation is essential.

Additionally, Rational Suite offers integrated environments for design, development, testing, and deployment, making it easier for teams to collaborate efficiently. Tools that facilitate communication and synchronization among team members support every project phase.

For example, when a developer checks in their code, the system automatically runs tests and generates reports, allowing other team members to review the results the next day. This automation enhances collaboration, speeds up development, and reduces manual overhead, improving overall productivity.

3. Version Control and Global Repositories: ClearCase

Effective collaboration relies on seamless coordination of code and version management. ClearCase has been an invaluable tool for this purpose.

ClearCase is a version control system that helps teams manage code development across multiple contributors. It ensures that:

• Different code versions are tracked

• Code is securely stored in a global repository

• Collaborators can work on different parts without conflicts

A key feature of ClearCase is its ability to allow developers to view specific parts of the code, modify them, and upload changes without conflicts. This ensures smooth collaboration and prevents overlapping work or unintended modifications.

Version control is especially critical in large collaborative environments, where multiple team members simultaneously work on different modules or features. ClearCase ensures that all changes are tracked, conflicts are identified, and integration is seamless, maintaining the project's integrity.

Its global repository feature further enhances collaboration by centralizing all software versions securely. This ensures teams can access the latest code, reducing miscommunication and confusion.

Whether teams are based in a single office or spread across continents, ClearCase ensures everyone is working on the same version of the project, fostering seamless collaboration.

4. Test Automation: Streamlining Development

Testing is an integral part of software development, and automating it can significantly enhance collaboration and productivity.

Previously, manual testing required extensive time and resources, often slowing development. However, test automation has revolutionized how teams approach testing and quality assurance.

Within the Rational Suite, several tools automate test script creation and execution. This ensures that:

• Tests are conducted regularly

• Results are automatically generated and shared with the team

For example, day builds and night tests have become standard practice in collaborative software environments.

• During the day, developers make changes to the codebase.

• At the end of the workday, the system automatically compiles the code into a new version.

• Overnight, automated test scripts run on the new build.

• By the next morning, developers receive detailed test reports highlighting potential issues.

This process enables continuous development and testing, identifying bugs and issues early. It also enhances collaboration by informing the team about the project's progress.

Developers can focus on coding without worrying about manual testing, while testers can review automated reports and address any concerns efficiently.

5. Integrated Development Environments: Eclipse

Another key tool that has evolved significantly is the Eclipse Integrated Development Environment (IDE).

Eclipse is an open-source IDE widely used by developers worldwide. It supports multiple programming languages and offers extensive integration capabilities.

One reason Eclipse has become a powerful collaboration tool is its seamless integration with:

• Version control systems like ClearCase

• Plugins for various development and testing tools

In a collaborative environment, Eclipse allows developers to work within a single, unified platform, enabling them to:

• Write, test, and debug code efficiently

• Manage version control within the same workspace

• Communicate and collaborate seamlessly with team members

This integration streamlines workflows, improves communication, and ensures everyone works in the same environment, minimizing discrepancies and inefficiencies.

Leveraging Tools to Foster a Collaborative Culture

The tools and methodologies I've highlighted—UML, Rational Suite, ClearCase, test automation, and Eclipse—are all integral to enhancing team collaboration.

However, the true success of collaboration is not just about using the right tools—it's about how these tools are implemented to foster a culture of teamwork and communication.

From my experience, the key to successful collaboration lies in:

• Providing teams with the right resources and support

• Encouraging open communication and knowledge sharing

• Creating a shared sense of responsibility

Access to these tools streamlined our workflow, ensuring everyone remained aligned.

• Communication flowed seamlessly

• Potential roadblocks were addressed proactively

• Project management tools kept us on track to meet our tight three-month deadline

Ultimately, the success of any project depends on efficient collaboration, and leveraging the right tools and processes ensures that teams work effectively, productively, and cohesively toward a shared vision.

I've always believed that having a solid process in place significantly increases the chances of success. It reduces the randomness that often plagues projects, especially in industries like software engineering, where individual work styles and flexible timelines can sometimes lead to inefficiency. By implementing a structured approach, we could bring out the best in every team member, regardless of their work preferences.

Happy Team = Effective Teamwork

One key lesson from this project is that teamwork is more than individuals coming together to complete a task. Effective teamwork requires synergy, where the group's collective effort amplifies each member's strengths. This project exemplified that.

The team members did not work in isolation. Instead, our group and our U.S. counterparts collaborated constantly. We held regular meetings to discuss progress, address issues, and align our efforts with the project objectives. Communication was clear, open, and constructive, allowing us to tackle problems before they escalated.

Moreover, the team members' enthusiasm was contagious. Everyone was genuinely invested in the project's success, which fostered a culture of support and mutual respect. As a result, the environment encouraged innovation and problem-solving. There were moments when challenges arose, but they were met with resilience and determination.

Maintaining motivation is essential to keeping a team productive and ensuring timely goal achievement. Team motivation stems from vision, leadership, company objectives, and professionalism. The team's integrity is vital and plays a crucial role in success. To achieve this, one must set clear goals, provide regular feedback, recognize achievements, encourage open communication, foster a positive work environment, offer growth opportunities, empower team members with autonomy, celebrate milestones, and actively listen to their concerns and needs.

By the project's final phase, we had completed the technology transfer, adapted the solution to a different platform, and implemented a robust product lifecycle management system in India. What initially seemed like an overwhelming task had been executed smoothly, thanks to the combined efforts of a highly skilled team, the right tools, and a well-structured process.

Looking back, this project stands out as one of the most successful in my career. Not only did we meet the client's expectations, but we also exceeded them, delivering a high-quality solution within the stipulated timeframe. The key takeaway from this experience is that teamwork can turn even the most challenging projects into success stories when combined with the right tools and processes.

It is not just about assembling a group of skilled professionals but about fostering a collaborative environment where everyone feels empowered to contribute.

Furthermore, the importance of having a structured process cannot be overstated. In a project with tight deadlines and multiple uncertainties, a well-defined process can provide the necessary stability and direction to guide the team toward success. The power of effective teamwork reminds us that no matter how daunting a task may seem, the right combination of people, processes, and tools can make all the difference.

Leadership as the Conductor

Leadership plays a critical role in orchestrating success, both in business and music. Just as a symphony conductor doesn't play any of the instruments but is essential in ensuring that each section of the orchestra performs harmoniously, a great business leader brings together their team's strengths, aligns them toward a shared vision, and guides them through challenges. The conductor's role is to listen, understand each musician's strengths and weaknesses, and adjust the tempo or dynamics to achieve the best possible performance.

In business, leaders act as facilitators, bringing together diverse talents within their organization and ensuring they work harmoniously toward a common goal. A great leader doesn't micromanage but trusts their team members to play their parts, stepping in only when necessary to provide guidance or adjust the strategy. The best leaders understand that their role is not to overshadow the team but to elevate them, empowering individuals to shine within the larger organization.

When I joined Philips, I quickly realized that my role as an innovation manager would be different from any position I had held before.

Unlike my previous roles in project management or technical leadership, where I worked with dedicated teams, this new role required me to act independently. There was no predefined innovation team waiting for me. Instead, I had to motivate people from different departments already engaged in other projects to think outside the box and contribute to innovative development.

Indirect Leadership

This shift was significant for me. My leadership responsibilities were clear-cut in my previous roles, and I had always worked with defined teams. But at Philips, the challenge was inspiring innovation across teams already deeply immersed in their daily work. I had to work with engineers and developers focused on routine projects and encourage them to explore advanced development, patent-worthy ideas, and disruptive technologies.

Indirect leadership involves influencing and guiding a team without directly overseeing their day-to-day work. It focuses on shaping the organization's vision, culture, and strategy, allowing team members to take ownership and make independent decisions. Instead of micromanaging, indirect leadership requires setting clear goals, providing support systems, empowering individuals, fostering collaboration, and ensuring effective organizational communication.

Key Ingredients of Indirect Leadership

• Communicate the vision, goals, and expectations to all team members, using various channels to ensure transparency.

• Explain the "why" behind decisions and provide necessary resources for team members to succeed.

• Identify and nurture potential leaders within the team, allowing them to take on more responsibility.

• Focus on results, not micromanagement—delegate tasks and hold individuals accountable for achieving outcomes rather than closely monitoring their daily activities.

• Recognize and celebrate achievements—publicly acknowledge individual and team accomplishments to boost morale and motivation.

• Provide constructive feedback—offer regular feedback to help individuals grow and develop their skills, emphasizing positive reinforcement and areas for improvement.

When Indirect Leadership is Most Effective

• **High-performing teams** – when team members have the necessary skills and experience to work autonomously.

• **Complex projects** – when collaboration across different departments and expertise is required.

• **Innovative environments** – where creativity and independent thinking are highly valued.

It was in this context that I learned the importance of indirect leadership. I had to build relationships, establish trust, and cultivate a sense of ownership among people who weren't officially part of my team. The key was to create an environment where they felt empowered to innovate. This required careful listening, understanding each person's motivations, and tailoring my approach to inspire them in ways that aligned with their goals.

In many ways, this role became more about mentorship and guidance than direct management, deepening my understanding of authentic leadership.

One of the earliest and most profound lessons I learned about fostering a collaborative environment was during the 1990s, when I worked on the Global Engineering Methodology Study (GEMS) project. This experience introduced me to the power of collaboration across time zones, leveraging global teams to ensure continuous development.

At the time, I was working with EDS, a prominent company. We were tasked with creating a teamwork environment that spanned three continents: Michigan in the United States, Bangalore in India, and Japan. The goal was ambitious yet straightforward—to develop a system where work could continue around the clock, taking advantage of time zone differences between locations.

The process worked seamlessly. The team in Michigan would begin their workday, make progress on the project, and log out and upload their work to a central repository by the end of their shift. The Bangalore team would then take over, building on the previous team's progress before passing it along to the team in Japan, who would complete their shift. This created a system of continuous development, ensuring that work never stopped. This collaborative approach reduced time-to-market and enabled us to overcome challenges faster.

However, creating this environment required more than just logistical coordination. It demanded the development of tools essential for global collaboration. Back then, we didn't have the advanced repositories or communication platforms we take for granted today. A crucial part of my role was to build a system that allowed us to share information securely and efficiently across continents. It was a profoundly enriching experience, highlighting the importance of collaboration between people and systems.

The Three C's of Technology: Computation, Communication, and Collaboration

When considering collaboration's role in any technological project, I often refer to the "Three C's of Technology: Computation, Communication, and Collaboration." Each serves as a pillar in the development of modern technology. Without a strong focus on collaboration, even the most powerful computational systems and advanced communication networks would struggle to deliver meaningful results.

Computation refers to the processing power that drives technological advancements. Following Moore's Law, processing speed and efficiency grow exponentially as hardware advances. However, computation alone is not enough.

The GEMS project began my journey toward understanding the essential role of technology in fostering collaboration. Today, we have an array of sophisticated tools—Zoom, Microsoft Teams, shared repositories, and cloud-based collaboration platforms—that make it easier than ever to work with people worldwide. These tools have become a fundamental part of the collaborative environments I strive to create in any workspace.

Enhancing collaboration within a team requires combining the right tools and methodologies. From planning and design to version control and testing, every phase of the software development lifecycle benefits from collaborative tools like UML, Rational Suite, and ClearCase.

These tools can drastically improve productivity and ensure project success when integrated into a well-structured collaborative environment.

Whether managing a team or contributing to a project, I strongly emphasize the effective use of these tools in my current roles. However, the tools themselves are not enough. It is how we use them and how we cultivate a mindset of open communication and shared responsibility that genuinely makes the difference.

The second pillar, Communication, is equally vital. Systems and people must interact seamlessly, sharing information across networks and between devices.

For example, a reliable communication platform is essential in a large organization where 50-60% of the staff may travel or work remotely. However, beyond having the right tools, a culture must encourage people to use these platforms to share ideas, provide feedback, and engage with their colleagues. Creating such a culture requires a few key principles: transparency, mutual respect, and a willingness to listen.

Open communication is also crucial. In my teams, I ensure everyone's voice is heard, regardless of their role or position. This approach not only fosters collaboration but also leads to better outcomes. When people feel their ideas are valued, they are more likely to contribute, and diverse perspectives often lead to more creative solutions.

The third pillar, Collaboration, brings everything together. Even in technology, systems must collaborate—whether processors coordinate tasks or teams collaborate to build, test, and refine products.

Trust is at the heart of any collaborative environment. When people trust each other, they are more willing to share ideas, take risks, and work together to solve problems. Fostering trust is one of my top priorities as a leader. I believe in allowing people to experiment, make mistakes, and learn from them. I encourage people to collaborate more openly and effectively by creating an environment where they feel supported and valued.

Collaboration is not just about leveraging the right tools; it is about cultivating an environment where communication flows freely and individuals feel empowered to contribute ideas.

Another critical lesson I've learned about collaboration is using time differences to our advantage. The GEMS project was the first time I saw this concept in action, and I continue to practice it today. One of the most significant benefits of working with global teams is ensuring that work never stops.

For instance, when working with a team in Europe and another in Australia, I can assign tasks to the European team at the end of their workday, knowing that when they log off, the Australian team will start their day. By the time I return to work the next morning, both teams will have made progress, keeping the momentum going. This 24/7 development cycle significantly reduces the time it takes to bring a product to market.

Again, the Three Cs—computation, Communication, and Collaboration—must be a strong foundation for this system. Each team must be able to seamlessly pick up where the other left off, which requires clear documentation, well-organized handoffs, and a shared understanding of the project's goals.

The Long-Term Impact of Collective Success

When businesses embrace the power of collaboration, they unlock the potential for long-term, sustainable success. While individual achievements may bring short-term gains, a team's ongoing collective effort has a lasting impact.

Teams that collaborate effectively can adapt more quickly to changes in the marketplace, pivot in response to challenges, and continuously innovate, keeping them ahead of the competition.

Innovation is often perceived as an individual pursuit, where solitary brilliance leads to groundbreaking discoveries. However, one of the most valuable lessons I have learned in my career is that some of the most significant innovations emerge from collective intelligence. When diverse minds collaborate—bringing their unique skills and perspectives to the table—they can solve challenges that might seem insurmountable when faced alone.

This was precisely the case when my team embarked on a mission to develop a device to help prevent blindness in premature babies. This story exemplifies how teamwork and collective intelligence can overcome seemingly impossible obstacles.

The challenge we faced was daunting. In India, more than 40 lakh (4 million) premature babies are born every year, and many are at risk of developing Retinopathy of Prematurity (ROP). This condition can lead to permanent blindness if not detected and treated early. Specialized retinal imaging is required for detection, but the available technology was prohibitively expensive.

At the time, a US-based company, Clarity Medical Systems, produced the only available camera, priced at over one crore rupees (approximately $120,000). This high cost made the device inaccessible to many hospitals in India, particularly rural areas. Moreover, its bulky nature meant it could only be used in well-equipped medical facilities, leaving many premature babies in remote locations without access to lifesaving screening.

Our mission was clear: develop a more affordable, portable, and efficient solution that could be widely deployed across India. But solving this problem required more than technical expertise—creativity, collaboration, and complementary skills.

From the outset, we knew that tackling this challenge would require expertise beyond our immediate team. Fortunately, we had the opportunity to collaborate with Dr. Anand, a pioneering pediatric ophthalmologist from Narayana Nethralaya, who had extensive experience treating premature babies at risk of blindness. His clinical insights were invaluable in defining the medical requirements for the device. However, despite this medical expertise, we faced numerous technical challenges, especially in optics, a field outside our core competencies.

Realizing the need for specialized knowledge, we contacted Calcutta University, where we connected with an optics and instrumentation expert, a Department of Applied Physics professor. This collaboration opened up new possibilities. With the professor's guidance and the contributions of two of his PhD students, our project evolved beyond a simple attempt to replicate the existing device—it became a truly innovative endeavor.

Innovation Through Diversity: Breaking the Mold

In the business world, diverse teams bring different perspectives and problem-solving approaches, helping to identify opportunities and challenges that a homogeneous group might overlook.

Teams with diverse skills, experiences, and viewpoints are better equipped to navigate complex, global challenges. Diversity fosters creativity, drives innovation, and pushes the boundaries of what is possible. In a world where markets and consumer needs evolve rapidly, businesses that can adapt, anticipate, and innovate are the ones that stay ahead—a task made easier when a variety of minds collaborate effectively.

At the outset, like many engineers, we initially thought within the constraints of what already existed. Our first instinct was to determine how to replicate the US-made device using cheaper materials and components. However, as we collaborated with the optics experts from Calcutta University, our thinking expanded. They challenged us to approach the problem differently, questioning the design principles of the original device and exploring alternative solutions.

For example, the original device used xenon lamps, which consumed excessive power and generated a lot of heat. Our collaborators proposed switching to LEDs, significantly reducing power consumption while making the device more compact and portable. This was just one of many insights that transformed our project from a simple duplication effort into a truly innovative solution.

Moreover, the US company that produced the original device had filed numerous patents to protect its intellectual property, creating additional barriers for us. However, with the support of our academic partners, we found ways to circumvent these patents by designing a device that worked on entirely different principles. This avoided legal complications, resulting in a cheaper, more efficient, and functionally superior device.

Collective Problem-Solving

As engineers, we were software, hardware design, and system integration experts, but lacked in-depth knowledge of optics and medical imaging. By collaborating with experts in medicine, optics, and academia, we combined our strengths and compensated for each other's weaknesses. This synergy was the key to overcoming the technical challenges that arose throughout the project.

In an isolated environment, we might have spent months or even years pursuing an idea that ultimately wouldn't work. But our assumptions were constantly tested in a collaborative setting, and we were challenged at every stage. We quickly learned whether an idea was viable, allowing us to move on to the next without wasting time. This iterative process saved us time and resources, enabling us to focus on ideas with real potential.

After months of collaboration and countless iterations, we finally developed an affordable, portable, compact, and energy-efficient device. Our final product, the 3nethra Neo, cost less than one-tenth of the original device and was small enough to be transported easily, even to remote areas. Its power consumption was a fraction of that of the original, making it more sustainable and easier to use in settings with limited access to electricity.

In terms of performance, the 3nethra Neo was just as effective as the US-made device, if not more so. It provided high-quality retinal images, allowing doctors to detect ROP in premature babies precisely.

More importantly, it made this life-saving technology accessible to hospitals and clinics across India, including in rural and underserved areas.

The 3nethra Neo has had a profound impact. By making retinal imaging more affordable and accessible, we have helped prevent blindness in countless premature babies who might otherwise have gone untreated. The device has also been recognized internationally, and we have filed multiple patents for the innovations we developed during the project.

What began as an attempt to duplicate an existing product evolved into a groundbreaking innovation, thanks to the collaboration of experts from different fields. Without the medical expertise of Dr. Anand, the optical insights from Calcutta University, and the engineering know-how of our team, the 3nethra Neo would never have come to fruition.

This experience taught me that the best innovations often arise when we challenge our assumptions, embrace diverse perspectives, and work together toward a common goal. The greatest takeaway from this experience is the power of collective intelligence. I carry this lesson with me in every project, knowing that collaboration is key to solving some of the world's most pressing challenges.

The Cost of Disunity: Learning from Failed Ventures

Fostering teamwork has implications beyond the immediate project at hand. When teams operate cohesively, they create a positive ripple effect. Successful collaborations lead to higher morale, more significant innovation, and a shared sense of purpose that drives future endeavors.

The success of any venture does not rely solely on individual talents or cutting-edge technology—it fundamentally depends on the collective strength of teamwork. Through my years of experience, I have witnessed a disheartening trend: many projects fail simply because they lack the critical ingredient of teamwork. The consequences of this deficiency are often severe, leading to wasted resources, damaged reputations, and lost opportunities.

Organizations that repeatedly fail due to lacking teamwork often struggle to attract and retain talent. The reputational damage deters potential collaborators, clients, and investors, creating a cycle of setbacks that becomes increasingly difficult to break.

How Organizations Can Avoid Failure

1. Cultivating a Culture of Teamwork

Organizations must prioritize cultivating a teamwork-oriented culture to prevent the pitfalls associated with disunity. This requires intentional efforts to break down silos, promote collaboration, and encourage open communication. Leadership plays a crucial role in modeling these behaviors and establishing norms that value teamwork.

For example, companies can implement regular team check-ins and collaborative brainstorming sessions, encouraging all members to share ideas and insights. Additionally, recognizing and celebrating collaborative successes fosters a sense of belonging and enables teams to work together more effectively.

Education also plays a vital role in shaping future generations of professionals. By emphasizing the importance of teamwork in academic settings, we can cultivate a workforce that values collaboration and understands its impact on success. This shift can be achieved through team-based projects, internships, and extracurricular activities, encouraging students to work together toward shared goals.

2. The Anatomy of Failure: Lack of Coordination

A project often begins with great enthusiasm and clear objectives, but as it progresses, the initial momentum can quickly dissipate when team members operate in silos. This lack of coordination manifests in various ways, primarily through ineffective communication and the entrenchment of individual egos. I have observed countless teams where members are more concerned with appeasing their managers or promoting their ideas than collaborating toward a common goal.

In one notable instance, I was involved in a software development project for a healthcare application to streamline patient data management. The team comprised talented individuals, each with unique expertise. However, rather than working collaboratively, they quickly fell into a pattern of individualism. One developer was focused on implementing new features, another on debugging, and a third was solely concerned with meeting deadlines. As a result, they failed to integrate their work effectively, leading to a fragmented application riddled with inconsistencies. When we finally attempted to bring all the components together, it became painfully clear that the lack of cohesive teamwork had resulted in a product that was far from functional.

The underlying issue in such scenarios is often a lack of shared vision. Without a unified understanding of project goals, team members may pursue their own paths, inadvertently creating a disjointed final product.

This phenomenon is particularly prevalent in environments where individual performance is heavily emphasized, such as corporate cultures that reward personal achievement over collaborative effort.

3. The Consequences of Individualism

Failing to foster teamwork can have catastrophic repercussions. In the healthcare application project, the inability to communicate effectively resulted in a failed product and a significant loss of stakeholder trust. Although initially backed by substantial funding and support, the project was ultimately scrapped. This loss was not just financial; it also set back the organization's timeline for implementing an essential service that could have improved patient care.

Moreover, this scenario highlights a fundamental truth: teamwork is not merely a "nice-to-have" but a "must-have." When team members prioritize personal agendas over collective goals, they jeopardize the project's success and the integrity of their professional relationships.

I have seen firsthand how resentment can brew in an environment where egos clash, leading to a toxic atmosphere that stifles innovation and creativity. Organizations that fail to recognize the importance of teamwork risk project failure and long-term damage to their reputation and work culture.

4. Recognizing the Warning Signs

Identifying early warning signs of disunity is crucial in preventing project failures. One standard indicator is when team members isolate themselves, forming cliques or exclusive circles that exclude others. This behavior often signifies a breakdown in communication and a shift toward individualistic thinking. In my experience, when teams lose sight of their shared mission, they become increasingly susceptible to failure.

Another warning sign is when the focus shifts from collaboration to competition. In one project, a marketing team was tasked with launching a new product. Instead of sharing insights and strategies, team members became more concerned with showcasing their ideas to management. This delayed the launch and diluted the impact of the marketing campaign, as the messaging became inconsistent and disjointed.

5. Learning from Mistakes: Successful Team Dynamics

While failures are regrettable, they also provide invaluable lessons. Reflecting on past projects, I've realized that successful teams share several key characteristics that mitigate the risks associated with disunity. These teams prioritize open communication, establish clear roles, and foster an environment of mutual respect.

For instance, during the development of a dialysis machine, our team faced challenges that could have easily led to failure. Engineers were tasked with designing and testing the equipment in the initial phases. However, when it came time for system-level tests, we invited technicians operating the machines in the field to participate in the testing process. Their insights proved critical in identifying flaws that the engineers had overlooked. This collaborative approach enhanced the machine's design and built a sense of ownership and respect among team members. Everyone understood the importance of their contributions, leading to a successful launch.

Furthermore, I've seen teams thrive in team-building activities that promote camaraderie and trust. When team members bond over shared experiences, they are more likely to collaborate effectively during projects. In one instance, a team I managed organized a retreat focused on problem-solving and communication exercises. The benefits of this investment became apparent during the subsequent project, where the team worked seamlessly together, leveraging each member's strengths and insights.

Navigating Team Conflicts

Conflict within a team is often seen as a stumbling block, a barrier that prevents progress and sows discord. However, conflict is not only inevitable but, when handled correctly, can catalyze growth and innovation. My experience navigating team conflicts has helped me understand that creating an environment that fosters open communication, humility, and a shared vision is key.

Understanding Conflict Dynamics

At the heart of every conflict lie many human emotions—pride, frustration, fear, and ego. When individuals feel their contributions are not recognized or their perspectives are overlooked, tensions can escalate. This is particularly true in environments where creativity and collaboration are crucial. In my work, I have witnessed how an unyielding focus on personal achievements can cloud judgment and lead to conflicts that undermine team cohesion.

To mitigate these issues, it's essential to establish a culture that prioritizes collective success over individual accolades. Recognizing the importance of each team member's input while addressing potential conflicts before they escalate has proven to be a cornerstone of effective teamwork.

Let us explore how to address and resolve conflicts to ensure they don't derail collective goals:

1. Proactive Conflict Prevention: The Power of Reviews

One of the most effective strategies I've implemented to preempt conflict is through regular reviews. During these sessions, we focus on what is going well and, more importantly, identify areas that need improvement. Creating a safe space where team members feel comfortable discussing challenges without fear of backlash is crucial.

To facilitate this process, I introduced the concept of Edward de Bono's "Six Thinking Hats" to our team. During the review process, each team member is assigned a different perspective. For instance, one might focus solely on project timing, while another scrutinizes costs. This structured approach allows us to analyze issues from various angles, diffusing personal biases and enabling us to view problems objectively.

The beauty of this method lies in its ability to remove the emotional weight often associated with critique. When team members wear metaphorical hats, they can distance themselves from their egos, fostering an atmosphere conducive to honest discussion and collaborative problem-solving. By rotating these roles, we ensure everyone experiences different viewpoints, ultimately enriching our understanding and decision-making.

2. Addressing Conflicts Head-On

Despite our best efforts, conflicts are sometimes unavoidable. When tensions arise, swift and decisive action is crucial to prevent the situation from escalating. My approach involves a few key steps:

• Acknowledging the conflict

• Facilitating open dialogue

• Fostering collaboration

One particularly memorable instance involved a project where two team leaders had conflicting ideas about the direction we should take. Instead of allowing the disagreement to fester, I arranged a meeting where both parties could express their views openly. I emphasized the importance of respectful listening, reminding the team that our ultimate goal was to serve the project, not win personal battles.

During the discussion, it became clear that both leaders had valid points, albeit from different perspectives. By encouraging them to focus on the project's needs rather than their individual preferences, we collectively brainstormed solutions that synthesized both ideas. This resolved the immediate conflict and strengthened the team's unity and shared purpose.

3. Avoid Being Egoistic in a Team

One of the biggest obstacles to resolving conflicts is the ever-persistent ego issue. In my experience, the more talented and accomplished a team member is, the more fragile their ego can become. This paradox often leads to defensiveness and a reluctance to collaborate.

During a visit to NASA, I learned an insightful lesson about managing ego in a high-pressure environment. As I chatted with a manager, he pointed to a dustbin labeled "EGO." He explained that every team member was encouraged to metaphorically "throw away" their egos upon entering the workplace. This concept resonated deeply with me.

By promoting the idea that personal pride should take a back seat to collective goals, we can create a culture where everyone feels valued without elevating their egos above the team's mission.

Implementing a similar strategy in my teams involved reminding members that our work was about more than just individual contributions. It was about harnessing our collective intelligence to achieve shared goals. Regular team-building activities and open forums for feedback reinforced this message, fostering an environment where humility was valued and collaboration flourished. 4. Encouraging Humility and Respect

Another critical aspect of conflict resolution is instilling a sense of humility and respect within the team. This doesn't mean downplaying individual contributions but rather encouraging team members to recognize the value of their colleagues' perspectives and experiences.

One practical approach is to celebrate collective successes. For instance, after completing a challenging project, I organized a gathering where team members could share their experiences and insights. Acknowledging individual efforts while framing them within the context of the team's success reinforces the idea that we are all together. By creating opportunities for team members to express gratitude and appreciation for one another, we cultivate a supportive atmosphere that diminishes ego-related conflicts.

Addressing and resolving conflicts extends beyond the immediate situation. When handled thoughtfully, these experiences can foster a culture of openness and resilience within the team. Team members learn that conflicts are not personal attacks but opportunities for growth and improvement. They become more adept at navigating challenges, and this agility translates into higher productivity and innovation.

Ultimately, conflict resolution is not merely about avoiding confrontation; it's about embracing it as a natural part of teamwork. By employing proactive strategies, facilitating open dialogue, managing egos, and fostering humility, we can ensure that conflicts do not derail our collective goals. Instead, they become stepping stones toward greater collaboration and success.

Evolving Understanding of Teamwork

My understanding and appreciation of teamwork have undergone significant transformation throughout my career. This evolution has been shaped by my experiences across various companies, from the pre-computer era of the late 1980s to today's tech-driven landscape. Reflecting on these experiences, I see a clear trajectory—from when teamwork was often synonymous with individual effort to an era where collaboration, communication, and collective innovation have become paramount.

When I embarked on my entrepreneurial journey in 1989, I entered a world vastly different from today's digitally connected environment. The landscape lacked advanced technology, communication was often limited, and the tools we relied upon were rudimentary at best. My first venture involved developing an anti-virus solution when computers emerged as essential business tools. Back then, teamwork was often an individual-driven endeavor.

Without sophisticated communication channels, success depended on trusting team members to take ownership of their responsibilities. The recruitment process was deeply personal; we sought individuals whose passion and commitment aligned with our vision. I often inquired about candidates' family backgrounds and previous experiences, looking for signs of dedication and reliability. In those early years, our success hinged on the strength of our interpersonal relationships and the collective determination of our team members.

Yet, while we had a strong sense of camaraderie and shared purpose, the limitations of our environment meant that we often operated in silos. Individual contributions were crucial, and there was little room for the commonplace collaborative processes today. The responsibility of leadership felt heavier, as there were fewer tools to facilitate teamwork and project management. This early experience taught me that while individual effort is vital, true success can only be achieved through unity and shared vision.

The Transformation: Embracing Technology and Collaborative Practices

As the years progressed, particularly in the late 1990s and early 2000s, I transitioned back into the corporate world, joining companies like Ericsson. This period marked a significant shift in my understanding of teamwork, primarily due to the advent of technology that revolutionized communication and collaboration. With the introduction of tools that facilitated project management and enhanced connectivity, our teams became more efficient and effective.

While at Ericsson, I witnessed firsthand how technology could bridge gaps between team members, fostering an environment conducive to collaboration. The availability of communication tools allowed us to share information seamlessly, enhancing our ability to work collectively toward common goals.

The experience reaffirmed my belief that teamwork requires a balance between human connection and technological support.

We developed diverse teams with a mix of skills and experiences, ensuring every project had a healthy combination of fresh talent and seasoned professionals. This diversity enhanced our ability to innovate and created a mentorship culture where knowledge was shared and nurtured. The changes I experienced in this corporate environment helped me appreciate that teamwork is not merely about working together; it is about leveraging each individual's strengths to create something more significant than the sum of its parts.

Navigating Challenges in the Age of Startups

Fast forward to today, and the landscape has continued to evolve, particularly with the rise of startups and a strong focus on innovation. While I admire the creativity and dynamism of these environments, I have also observed a concerning trend toward individualism. Many startups operate under the impression that each team member must embody the role of an innovator, leading to a proliferation of ideas that often lack cohesion.

This shift toward individualism poses a significant challenge to effective teamwork. While innovation is essential, it must be harnessed within a framework of shared goals and disciplined execution. When team members become overly focused on their ideas, it can lead to fragmentation and distraction from the project's primary objectives. Managing diverse opinions and ensuring alignment with a unified vision has become one of the most pressing challenges in contemporary teamwork.

Moreover, the abundance of tools and platforms available today can sometimes overwhelm team members, making it difficult to determine which resources to use for collaboration. The principle of "choice paralysis" often applies, where having too many options leads to confusion and reduced effectiveness. In an era where individuals can easily become isolated due to remote work or freelance arrangements, reinforcing the importance of collaboration as a foundational element of success is crucial.

The Necessity of Discipline and Structure

After years in business and corporate environments, I have realized that discipline and structure are essential to successful teamwork. Established frameworks ensure adherence to specific processes and standards in the corporate world, especially within larger organizations. These structures provide clarity and direction, keeping team members aligned and working toward common objectives.

In contrast, startup culture can sometimes lack this discipline, as flexibility and rapid iteration are often prioritized over established processes. While I appreciate startups' creativity and speed, I also recognize that teams can quickly lose their way without a solid structure. Discipline in project management, communication, and accountability is crucial to harnessing the full potential of teamwork.

The COVID-19 pandemic has introduced new dimensions to teamwork, as remote work has become the norm for many organizations. This shift has underscored the need for practical collaboration tools and well-defined team practices. My experiences during this period have highlighted that even when team members are physically apart, they can still work cohesively if equipped with the right tools and a shared commitment to the project's success.

Building a Collaborative Culture for the Future

As I look to the future, fostering a collaborative culture will be paramount. This involves encouraging open communication, building trust, and recognizing each team member's strengths. By prioritizing collaboration over individualism, we can create environments where creativity flourishes, ideas are shared freely, and teams work together to overcome challenges.

Behind every successful venture lies a team that has worked together, navigated challenges, and celebrated achievements. The journey to success is rarely a solitary endeavor but a collective effort built on collaboration, communication, and a shared vision. When individuals unite with a common purpose, they create a powerful synergy that amplifies their strengths and mitigates their weaknesses. This unity is essential in today's fast-paced and ever-evolving business landscape.

Embracing the spirit of teamwork is not just a strategy for success—it is the foundation upon which innovation and progress are built. Teams that foster a culture of collaboration are better equipped to generate creative solutions, adapt to changing circumstances, and respond to challenges with agility. When diverse perspectives are welcomed and valued, the team can think more creatively, leading to breakthroughs that would be impossible in isolation.

Teamwork is about sharing tasks and creating an environment where everyone feels valued and empowered to contribute to the project's success.

3

EMPATHY IN ACTION

"Leadership is not about being in charge. It's about taking care of those in your charge."

– Simon Sinek

L et's imagine a customer who feels frustrated due to a disappointing service experience and contacts the company to address the issue. Instead of receiving a standard, automated response, they are met with a heartfelt apology and a personalized solution. This interaction not only resolves the issue but also transforms the customer into a loyal advocate for the brand. This is the power of empathy in action.

Often regarded as a soft skill reserved for personal relationships, empathy rapidly emerges as a critical asset in business. Understanding and sharing another's feelings is a moral virtue and a strategic advantage. In today's competitive landscape, businesses prioritize empathy to foster genuine connections, drive innovation, build loyalty, and achieve tremendous success.

Consider the story of Zappos, the online shoe retailer renowned for its exceptional customer service. When a customer called to return shoes that didn't fit, the representative didn't just process the return.

Upon learning that the shoes were for a wedding that had to be canceled due to a family emergency, the representative went above and beyond, sending a sympathy card and flowers on behalf of the company. This act of empathy not only won the customer's heart but also garnered widespread admiration and loyalty for Zappos.

Similarly, Howard Schultz, the former CEO of Starbucks, demonstrated empathy during a critical time in the company's history. Amid declining sales and a demotivated workforce, Schultz prioritized personally reconnecting with employees and customers. His empathetic approach revitalized the company's culture, inspiring employees and leading to a significant turnaround in performance.

This chapter will explore the multifaceted nature of empathy and its profound impact on business and entrepreneurship. We will delve into real-life stories of leaders and companies that have harnessed empathy to achieve remarkable outcomes. By examining the components of empathy, its benefits, and practical ways to cultivate it, we aim to demonstrate that empathy is not just a nice-to-have but a must-have for anyone aspiring to lead in today's business environment.

Empathy as a Strategic Advantage in Business

Empathy is more than just a soft skill; it has become a critical asset in modern business and entrepreneurship. It lays the foundation for genuine relationships, informed decision-making, and transformative leadership.

Empathy is essential in today's competitive market, especially in product development. One instance where an empathetic approach significantly impacted our business was during the development of a pediatric ophthalmology device specifically for neonatal care.

The challenge we sought to address was retinopathy of prematurity (ROP)—a condition that puts premature babies at risk of blindness if not diagnosed and treated within the first few weeks of life.

Given the sensitive and complex nature of the healthcare sector, my team and I knew we could not directly experience the challenges these babies, their caregivers, and medical professionals face. However, we understood that gathering insights from key stakeholders would be crucial in designing a solution that genuinely met their needs.

We began by stepping into the shoes of the various stakeholders involved. First, we empathized with the mothers of premature babies, many of whom came from rural areas. For them, traveling to major cities for screening and treatment was a significant obstacle. Next, we considered the pediatric ophthalmologists and the healthcare system, which needed to deliver timely care but struggled due to a lack of accessible medical equipment. While some devices existed for screening ROP, they were prohibitively expensive and primarily located in large metropolitan areas, making them inaccessible to rural families.

To gain deeper insights, our team of five design engineers spent extensive time interviewing doctors, caregivers, and hospital administrators to understand the intricacies of these challenges.

They asked critical questions such as:

• What are the biggest obstacles to early detection?

• What resources do families need to access care?

• How can we make the treatment process faster and more efficient?

After a thorough investigation, we identified several critical issues. The first was accessibility—existing devices were too expensive and available only in urban areas. The second was transportation—many families struggled to travel long distances to specialized hospitals. The third was timing—there is only a six-week window to detect and treat ROP. Missing this window often meant permanent blindness for many newborns.

We pinpointed the core pain points that needed solving by empathizing with all the involved parties. We set out to develop a portable, affordable, and effective device in rural settings. Our team worked tirelessly, driven by the understanding that every day we delayed meant more babies at risk of losing their eyesight. Our urgency and emotional connection with the problem accelerated our development timeline. Typically, a project of this magnitude would take much longer, but empathy ignited a fire within the team, inspiring them to work day and night.

Ultimately, we created a product that costs a fraction of the price of imported devices and is easily transportable to rural areas. Since its launch, this device has been deployed in multiple neonatal intensive care units (NICUs) across the country and neighboring nations, helping prevent blindness in thousands of babies annually.

This example underscores how empathy can transform product development and address pressing societal issues. By genuinely understanding the needs of those you aim to serve, you can create solutions that meet functional requirements and alleviate real human suffering. For us, empathy was the catalyst for innovation, accelerating our progress and ensuring our product made a meaningful difference in the world.

We didn't just create a viable product through this empathetic approach—we built a system that prioritizes people's needs, particularly the most vulnerable. This is the power of empathy—it's not just a design tool; it's a driving force that leads to impactful solutions for real-world problems.

Challenges in Promoting Empathy Within a Corporate or Business Environment

Promoting empathy in corporate and business environments presents unique challenges, especially when comparing the approaches of startups and large multinational corporations. Having worked in both worlds, I have encountered several barriers that must be navigated when fostering a culture of empathy.

1. Understanding the Difference Between Empathy and Sympathy

One key challenge in promoting empathy within large corporate environments is the confusion between empathy and sympathy. In big companies, employees often sympathize with problems rather than empathize. While sympathy is well-intentioned, it creates distance between the person offering help and those in need.

For example, when someone sees hunger, their reaction might be to donate food or money, offering a short-term solution. While generous, this approach is rooted in sympathy and distances the person from the root cause of the problem. It often reinforces a divide between those offering help and those receiving it.

Empathy, on the other hand, requires a deeper level of connection. It involves truly understanding the other person's struggles by stepping into their shoes. An empathetic response would involve asking, "What can I do to help this person sustain?" Instead of just offering food, an empathetic approach might explore long-term solutions like helping individuals develop skills or start micro-businesses, empowering them to solve their problems.

Distinguishing between empathy and sympathy is crucial, yet instilling this understanding in large corporate environments remains challenging. Encouraging employees to go beyond surface-level solutions and truly engage with problems on a human level requires a fundamental shift in mindset—one that many organizations struggle to implement.

2. Corporate Culture and Disconnect

Corporate environments, especially in large multinational companies, often present challenges due to their structure. Employees, particularly young engineers or executives, experience a certain level of "pampering" when they enter the corporate world. They receive high salaries, generous benefits, and numerous perks that gradually distance them from the real-world struggles faced by customers, patients, or end-users.

This disconnect makes it difficult for employees to empathize with those they should serve. Many companies encourage employees to engage in social work, such as visiting schools or healthcare centers on weekends. While commendable, these efforts often result in acts of sympathy rather than genuine empathy. Employees may participate in charitable activities, donate money, or volunteer their time, but they rarely take the time to understand the root causes of the issues they are addressing.

3. Startups and Empathy: A Different Mindset

In contrast, startups often cultivate a greater capacity for empathy within their teams. This is primarily because startups face significant challenges, including financial constraints, resource limitations, and the constant need to stay agile in a competitive market. This struggle fosters a firsthand understanding of hardship, making team members more attuned to the struggles of their end-users.

Unlike large corporations, startups are closely connected to their customers' pain points. They cannot afford to offer superficial solutions; to survive, they must address the root causes of problems. This direct engagement makes empathy a powerful tool for innovation, allowing startups to create meaningful, user-centric solutions rather than merely applying short-term fixes.

4. Training and Artificial Empathy in Corporates

Promoting empathy in large corporations often requires structured training programs to help employees better understand the problems they are trying to solve. However, despite these initiatives, empathy in corporate environments can often feel artificial. Employees may go through the motions of showing empathy without truly internalizing its significance.

This lack of genuine empathy becomes especially problematic in industries like healthcare, where understanding patients' needs is essential to developing practical solutions. Large corporations, driven by scalability and profitability, often focus on high-cost solutions rather than tailoring their products and services to the real needs of the people they serve. As a result, many corporate-led innovations fail to reach the communities that need them most.

5. Impact on Industries Like Healthcare

The challenges of promoting empathy within large corporations are particularly evident in industries like healthcare, where empathy is crucial to delivering effective and accessible solutions. While startups prioritize affordability and user-centered design, large corporations develop complex, high-end products that often remain financially or logistically out of reach for those in rural or underserved areas.

For example, major healthcare companies frequently invest in developing cutting-edge medical equipment with advanced features that increase costs, making them unaffordable for many hospitals and clinics in lower-income regions. In contrast, startups are more likely to focus on cost-effective, scalable solutions because they are closer to the patients and healthcare providers who struggle with accessibility issues daily.

Shifting from Sympathy to Genuine Empathy

Promoting empathy in corporate environments is a complex challenge, especially compared to startups' more agile and personal approach. The confusion between empathy and sympathy, the disconnect created by corporate culture, and the need for training to instill genuine empathy are all significant barriers.

While startups often embody empathy naturally due to their direct connection with users and shared struggles, larger corporations frequently fall into the sympathy trap, leading to superficial solutions rather than impactful change.

The Need for a Cultural Shift

Large companies must undergo a cultural shift to harness the power of empathy. They must move away from distant acts of charity or goodwill toward a more connected, empathetic approach. Instead of merely offering donations or CSR initiatives, organizations must engage deeply with their communities, listen actively, and develop solutions tailored to real-world challenges.

Empathy is a moral virtue and a key driver of innovation and meaningful problem-solving. Organizations genuinely embracing empathy will be better positioned to create a lasting impact and foster deeper customer loyalty, trust, and long-term success.

Case Study of Dr. Venkataswamy, founder of Aravind Eye Care, and Dr. R. A. Mashelkar, a visionary in science and technology.

Empathetic leadership is a key quality that enables leaders to connect more deeply with their teams, customers, and communities. It fosters innovation, inclusiveness, and social responsibility. Two leaders stand out for their profound contributions to their fields and exemplify empathy in their leadership styles: Dr. Venkataswamy, founder of Aravind Eye Care, and Dr. R. A. Mashelkar, a visionary in science and technology.

Dr. Venkataswamy – Founder of Aravind Eye Care

Dr. Venkataswamy, affectionately known as Dr. V, is renowned for his empathetic leadership in the healthcare sector. His vision to make high-quality eye care accessible and affordable for everyone, especially the underprivileged, is a testament to his deep empathy for society's most vulnerable.

After retiring from military service as a doctor, he shifted his focus to addressing the need for affordable eye care, which led to the founding of the Aravind Eye Care System. This system is now one of the largest providers of eye care globally.

Affordable Eye Care through Cross-Subsidization: Dr. Venkataswamy implemented a business model that ensures those who can afford care pay for themselves and others who cannot. This cross-subsidization model allows free or heavily discounted care for impoverished patients while maintaining high medical treatment standards. This approach reflects his understanding that empathy means creating long-term, sustainable solutions rather than short-term fixes.

Empathy through Local Talent Development: Dr. V focused on reducing the cost of eye surgeries and creating opportunities for local employment. He trained local nurses, often young women who had only passed the 10th standard, turning them into skilled healthcare professionals. These nurses, coming from the same socio-economic backgrounds as their patients, could deeply empathize with their needs. This initiative not only reduced healthcare costs but also empowered local communities.

Innovation with Empathy: The high cost of importing intraocular lenses was a significant challenge in affordable eye care. Recognizing this as a barrier for patients, Dr. V led efforts to develop the technology for producing these lenses locally. By securing technology transfers from the United States and collaborating with charitable institutions, Aravind Eye Care could manufacture lenses in India, drastically lowering costs while maintaining quality. This innovative approach showed empathy in caring for patients and addressing the systemic economic challenges they faced.

Global Impact: Aravind Eye Care has revolutionized eye care in India and expanded its reach globally. The organization trains healthcare professionals in countries like Africa and China, enabling these regions to provide eye care locally without requiring patients to travel great distances. This global outreach highlights Dr. Venkataswamy's empathy in understanding the need for accessible healthcare for all, regardless of geographical location.

Dr. R. A. Mashelkar – Pioneer in Science and Technology

Dr. R. A. Mashelkar is another leader who exemplifies empathetic leadership through his contributions to science, technology, and innovation. He came from a humble background to become India's Director General of the Council of Scientific & Industrial Research (CSIR). His approach to leadership is centered on understanding the unique challenges faced by his country and its people and innovating solutions that address these needs.

Key Contributions:

Creating Specialized Research Centers: Dr. Mashelkar's leadership resulted in establishing various specialized CSIR labs across India, each focusing on solving specific problems unique to its region. For instance, the Bhavnagar lab specializes in converting hard water from the sea into drinkable soft water—a critical need in water-scarce areas. These labs address local problems while applying advanced scientific research, demonstrating his empathetic understanding of regional challenges and his commitment to addressing them.

Empathy in Scientific Innovation: Dr. Mashelkar's remarkable contribution is promoting innovation that directly benefits society.

He emphasized "social engineering" and focused on creating cutting-edge technologies and scientific breakthroughs that were socially impactful. For example, at the National Chemical Laboratory (NCL) in Pune, he established an entrepreneurship center focused on fostering science and technology startups. This step empowered young entrepreneurs to address societal challenges using science as a tool, bridging the gap between high-tech innovations and real-world needs.

Championing Intellectual Property Rights with Empathy: Dr. Mashelkar was pivotal in transforming India's intellectual property rights (IPR) approach. He understood that India's reliance on patented foreign drugs and technologies created barriers to local innovation. To counter this, he fostered a healthy culture of patenting within India. However, his approach to patenting was also empathetic—he argued that natural and ancient knowledge should not be patented. For instance, he advocated against patenting traditional Indian knowledge like turmeric or neem, ensuring that such knowledge remained accessible to all.

Empathy for Socio-Economic Development: Dr. Mashelkar's empathy extends beyond science and technology. He has been deeply involved in ensuring scientific progress contributes to the nation's socioeconomic development. Whether creating new water treatment solutions, reducing dependency on patented drugs, or fostering entrepreneurship, he has continually sought to balance technological advancement with social responsibility.

Dr. Venkataswamy and Dr. R. A. Mashelkar exemplify what it means to be an empathetic leader.

Dr. V's pioneering work in affordable healthcare and Dr. Mashelkar's transformative contributions to science and technology highlight their commitment to addressing societal challenges through innovative, empathetic approaches. They both demonstrate that authentic leadership is not just about managing teams or scaling organizations; it is about understanding the needs of the people they serve and creating solutions that empower those individuals to improve their lives sustainably and meaningfully.

Integrating Empathy into Business Core Values and Practices

Empathy is a foundational element of successful business practices today. It ensures that products and services are designed for functionality and with the end users' real needs, emotions, and experiences at the center. Integrating empathy into a business's core values and operations requires a multifaceted approach, where user-centric design, active listening, and employee engagement play critical roles. Below is a framework for embedding empathy into business practices based on real-world insights.

1. User-Centric Approach and Design Thinking

At the heart of empathetic business practices lies a user-centric approach that places the customer or end user at the center of every decision to ensure that the product or service directly addresses their needs, desires, and pain points.

Design Thinking as a Tool for Empathy: Design thinking is one of the most effective frameworks for integrating empathy into business practices. This methodology involves deeply understanding the user's perspective by immersing oneself in their environment, challenges, and experiences. Businesses that adopt design thinking prioritize user feedback at the beginning of the product development process. Rather than assuming what users need, they ask the right questions and observe user behaviors to gain authentic insights.

Mapping User Journeys: A key practice in the design thinking process is mapping the user journey, which helps businesses track and analyze every touchpoint of a user's interaction with their product or service. By documenting each stage of the user experience, businesses can identify potential pain points and areas for improvement.

More importantly, when employees actively immerse themselves in this journey, they develop a deeper understanding of user struggles, fostering a culture of empathy that leads to better, user-focused solutions.

2. Usability Testing and Feedback Loops

Understanding user needs is not a one-time event but an ongoing process. By incorporating usability testing as a standard business practice, organizations ensure that empathy remains at the core of their product and service development.

Usability Labs: One effective method for sustaining user empathy is through usability labs, where users interact with prototypes or existing products while their behaviors and feedback are recorded. This process enables engineers and designers to observe how real users interact with their products in a controlled environment. A single-sided mirror technique is often used, allowing engineers to observe users without interfering, ensuring that reactions and insights are captured without bias or influence.

Listening over Dictating: A crucial aspect of usability testing is prioritizing listening over directing. Simply asking users for feedback is not enough—businesses must actively listen and observe behaviors without imposing preconceived notions. Genuine empathy in business means understanding user needs without influencing their opinions. This approach ensures the resulting value proposition is authentic and aligned with user expectations.

3. Cross-Verification and Iterative Development

Once businesses gain initial insights and develop products or services, the next critical step is cross-verifying these insights with real users. This process ensures that empathy remains central throughout the entire development lifecycle.

Sample Verification: Before fully launching a product or finalizing a value proposition, businesses should conduct sample testing with a representative group of users to validate whether it meets their needs. This ensures that assumptions are not driving development and that user feedback continues to shape the product. If test users identify gaps or issues, businesses can make necessary adjustments, ensuring that final solutions resonate with the target audience.

Iterative Product Development: Empathy in business is not about creating a one-size-fits-all solution from the outset but about remaining flexible and adaptable as more user insights emerge. Adopting an iterative development approach, businesses can continuously refine and improve their products based on real-world feedback. This process ensures sustained relevance, long-term customer satisfaction, and increased brand loyalty.

4. Fostering an Empathy-Driven Team Culture

Empathy isn't just a top-down strategy imposed by leadership—it must be embraced at every level of an organization, from engineers and designers to customer service representatives.

Involving Engineers in the Process: Engineers are often considered the backbone of product development. To maintain an empathetic approach, they must be directly involved in understanding the user experience. Encouraging engineers to spend time in the field and actively engage with users enables them to empathize with customers' challenges. This hands-on involvement ensures that empathy is not just a theoretical concept but a practical practice that shapes product design and development.

Maintaining a Human Connection: One risk of designing with empathy is that, over time, team members may distance themselves emotionally from users as the process becomes routine. Organizations must foster a culture where employees are constantly reminded to maintain their human connection with users to prevent this. Empathy requires continuous reinforcement; teams must focus on user experiences rather than treating people as data points or subjects in a usability study.

5. Systematic Empathy Models

Empathy can be applied at both the individual and group levels. Businesses can implement various systematic techniques to embed empathy into their processes, ensuring it remains a core element of operations.

Individual and Group Empathy: While individual empathy focuses on the direct emotional understanding between a team member and a user, group empathy considers the collective experience of a team. Both are essential. Individuals must feel personally connected to users, but the entire organization must align with this commitment to empathy.

One effective technique is empathy mapping workshops, where teams visualize the user's emotions, pain points, and thoughts. These exercises help align the team toward empathetic decision-making and ensure user-centric thinking is at the heart of every project.

Integrating empathy into a business's core values and practices is an ongoing process that requires thoughtful design, user-centric approaches, continuous feedback, and an engaged team. Businesses can create better products and stronger, long-term customer relationships by incorporating empathy-driven strategies, such as design thinking, usability testing, feedback loops, and fostering a human connection. The key is to remain flexible, open to listening, and committed to prioritizing users in every decision.

The Importance of Empathy in Problem-Solving

Empathy is vital to problem-solving, particularly in fields focusing on human well-being. A lack of empathy can lead to misjudgments, poorly designed solutions, and conflicts. One striking example occurred during a medical screening camp, where insufficient empathy resulted in significant challenges.

In this instance, a healthcare team organized ophthalmology screening camps for local communities to check for common eye-related issues, such as cataracts and refractive errors. The program was widely successful because the community was familiar with and comfortable with these screenings. Over time, the team decided to expand the scope of these camps by including screenings for non-communicable eye diseases, such as diabetic retinopathy and glaucoma.

This incremental change was well-received because it aligned with the community's needs and expectations. The eye screenings focused on issues the local population understood, addressing approximately 85% of common eye problems.

The Problem: Expanding to Kidney Disease Screening

Buoyed by the success of the expanded eye screenings, the team sought to maximize the utility of these camps even further. They proposed adding kidney disease screening, specifically for chronic kidney disease (CKD), assuming it could be seamlessly integrated into the existing eye camps. The logic behind this expansion was that since people were already coming for eye screenings, adding kidney screenings would be an efficient use of resources.

However, this assumption proved to be deeply flawed.

Why Does a Lack of Empathy Lead to Failure?

The kidney disease screening initiative failed because the team did not fully empathize with the participants' context and needs. The primary issue was that kidney disease screening requires urine sample collection, a process fundamentally incompatible with the infrastructure and setup of the existing eye screening camps.

Mismatch in Logistics: Unlike eye screenings, which are quick and noninvasive, kidney screenings require collecting and handling urine samples—a process that demands proper facilities, including toilets, hygiene supplies, and privacy. However, many people attending the screening camps came from rural areas or temporary settlements where proper sanitation facilities were scarce or nonexistent. Sometimes, these communities lacked basic infrastructure, making urine sample collection impractical.

Failure to Consider the User Journey: The team assumed that since people were already attending the eye screenings, they could also easily participate in kidney screenings. However, they failed to consider the user journey. For an older person or a resident of a temporary slum, walking into a camp for an eye checkup is one thing, but providing a urine sample under inadequate conditions is an entirely different challenge. The team's lack of empathy for the specific environment and barriers faced by the community, especially concerning sanitation, meant that the kidney screening effort was doomed from the start.

Sympathy vs. Empathy: The Critical Difference

In this case, the team demonstrated sympathy by recognizing the need for kidney disease screenings. However, sympathy alone was not enough. Genuine empathy was lacking, which requires understanding the user's context, environment, and feelings.

The team sympathized with the problem (the need for kidney screenings) but did not fully grasp how the community members would experience the screening process, given their living conditions.

This lack of understanding led to a poorly designed solution that failed to account for the target population's daily struggles. The result was a failed screening effort, wasted resources and time, and potential frustration and discomfort for participants, who may have felt inconvenienced or humiliated by the setup.

Learning and Corrective Action: Adjusting the Approach

Recognizing their mistake, the team had to rethink their strategy. They realized that kidney screening could not be conducted in the same manner as eye screenings. Instead, they devised an alternative method—door-to-door screening, which was far more practical for collecting urine samples.

New Method: The revised approach involved creating a kit with a urine sample collector, which was distributed to individuals in their homes. This allowed participants to provide samples in a more private and comfortable setting, while health workers later collected the samples for testing.

Walking the User Journey: This experience was a valuable lesson in understanding the user's journey. Had the team initially imagined themselves in the participants' shoes, as an older person in a village or living in a slum without proper sanitation, they might have avoided this failure. Empathy requires designing for the user and experiencing the problem from their perspective.

By observing, listening to, and understanding the user in their context, the team would have recognized the impracticality of combining kidney screenings with eye camps early on.

Empathy as the Key to Problem Solving

This situation underscores the crucial role of empathy in design thinking. Without it, even well-intentioned efforts can miss the mark. The key takeaway is that when designing any service or solution, particularly in healthcare, it's essential to:

Deeply Understand the Environment: In this case, a more profound understanding of the community's living conditions, sanitation challenges, and cultural norms would have revealed the need for a different approach from the outset.

Listen and Observe: Empathy is not just about listening to what people say, but also observing how they live and interact with their surroundings. The team failed to fully observe and engage with participants' realities, resulting in a flawed solution.

Adapt Solutions to Fit the User's Context: Ultimately, empathy means designing solutions that align with the user's unique circumstances. By shifting to door-to-door screenings and providing sample collection kits, the team demonstrated adaptability in addressing the community's specific needs and challenges.

The failure of the initial kidney screening effort, due to a lack of empathy, highlights an essential lesson in business and healthcare:

Empathy is not just about understanding the problem—it's about understanding the people affected by it, their environment, limitations, and needs. Even seemingly simple challenges can become significant obstacles when businesses and teams fail to empathize. In contrast, an empathy-driven approach leads to more effective, sustainable solutions that genuinely serve the people they are designed to help.

Training and Encouraging Empathy in Teams

Empathy is essential for developing meaningful and practical solutions, especially when designing products or services for underserved communities. Training a team to adopt empathetic practices can be transformative, ensuring that solutions genuinely address the needs and challenges of the people they aim to help. Here's how a team can cultivate empathy using immersive techniques, keen observation, and data-driven insights.

1. Immersive Training: Understanding the Context

Immersion is a powerful method for training teams in empathy. This approach encourages team members to engage actively with the communities they serve, helping them understand challenges firsthand. Similar to how a politician embarks on a padayatra (foot journey) to connect with people from different regions and demographics, immersion allows innovators to experience the lives of their target users directly.

Immersion as a Tool: Immersive techniques involve placing team members in resource-constrained environments, where they live with the people they are designing solutions for. This firsthand experience enables them to understand daily struggles better and develop contextual solutions.

For example, if a team is developing a healthcare solution for rural populations, they would spend time living in a village, observing and participating in daily activities to gain a genuine understanding of the environment.

Experiencing Problems Firsthand: When a team member walks through the user journey and "lives in their shoes," they develop a deeper emotional connection to the real constraints, struggles, and emotions of the people they aim to serve. This hands-on approach builds authentic empathy, making it far more effective than just studying reports or conducting interviews.

2. Keen Observation: The Foundation of Empathy

Empathy cannot be cultivated without keen observation skills. Training teams to be active observers is critical in fostering genuine empathy. This involves listening to what people say and watching how they live, work, and solve problems in their environment.

• Active Listening and Watching: Team members must learn to be attentive observers, paying close attention to how people interact with their surroundings and each other. This includes:

o Noticing nonverbal cues and unspoken struggles.

o Identifying barriers that people may not explicitly express.

o Understanding the broader social and cultural context in which people navigate daily challenges.

• Recording and Reflecting: Observations should be documented systematically, ensuring structured insights.

o The team must be trained to analyze, reflect, and extract key insights from their immersion experience.

o Reviewing these observations allows for deeper understanding and ensures solutions remain user-centered.

3. The Role of Data and Research

While immersion and observation establish an emotional connection with the target community, data and research help validate and scale those insights. A blend of qualitative and quantitative research ensures that teams address real and significant problems.

Balancing Quantitative and Qualitative Insights:

• Quantitative data (e.g., statistics, survey results) helps define the scale of the problem.

• Qualitative insights (e.g., personal experiences, testimonials) deepen understanding and provide rich context.

Using Data to Inform Empathy:

While data highlights the numbers, immersion brings them to life. Teams must be trained to combine both approaches, ensuring their solutions are scalable and deeply relevant.

4. Walking Through the User Journey: Developing Connection

Empathy requires more than just listening or observing—it demands walking through the user's journey and understanding their emotional, physical, and environmental context. This step helps team members connect with the people they are designing for on a deeper level.

Understanding the Journey: Teams should be trained to imagine themselves in their users' shoes.

For example, when designing a solution for an older person in a rural village, they need to think about the entire experience—

• How does this person experience their day?

• What are their most significant challenges and fears?

• What would make their life easier?

Creating Real Connections: Building a genuine connection with the people you serve allows team members to internalize their struggles, leading to more thoughtful, creative, and user-centric solutions.

These connections often reveal hidden pain points that data or interviews might miss.

5. The Role of Passion: Driving Authentic Empathy

Empathy cannot be manufactured or imposed—it must come from genuine passion. A key element in training a team to adopt empathetic practices is ensuring that team members genuinely care about the problems they are solving.

Selecting Passionate Team Members:

• Empathy training begins with selecting the right individuals.

• Choosing team members who are passionate about the cause and motivated to make a difference is essential.

• A person driven by passion is likelier to go the extra mile to understand the user and find creative, empathetic solutions.

Encouraging Authenticity: Authenticity in empathy comes when teams are encouraged to embrace their passion and connect with users on a human level.

This connection goes beyond professional obligations—it's about caring deeply for the person behind the problem.

6. Building Skills: Observation, Listening, and Documentation

Training a team to adopt empathetic practices requires developing key observation, listening, and documentation skills.

Training in Observation: Team members need to be taught how to be keen observers.

This involves:

• Noticing details, interpreting non-verbal cues, and understanding body language and context.

• Uncovering hidden insights that are not immediately obvious but are critical to designing effective solutions.

Training in Listening: Listening isn't just about hearing what someone says; it's about understanding the meaning behind their words.

Teams should be trained to:

• Listen actively, ask the right questions, and seek to understand the emotional context of a user's words.

Training in Documentation: Structured documentation ensures that insights gained through immersion and observation are not lost.

Team members must be trained to:

• Thoroughly and systematically document findings for practical reflection and analysis.

By incorporating these principles, businesses can embed empathy into their culture, design processes, and customer interactions, ultimately leading to more impactful and sustainable solutions.

7. Empathy as a Mindset: The Long-Term Approach

Empathy isn't just a one-time training but a mindset that needs to be nurtured over time. Teams should be encouraged to internalize empathy in every project and view it as a fundamental aspect of problem-solving.

• **Continuous Reflection:** Teams should be encouraged to regularly reflect on their experiences, asking themselves how their work impacts the people they serve. This reflection fosters a culture where empathy is a continuous practice, rather than a task checked off during project development.

• **Encouraging Empathy at Every Step:** Whether at the planning, design, or execution stage, empathy should guide decision-making throughout the process. This long-term approach ensures that user-centric design is deeply embedded in the team's culture.

Training a team to adopt empathetic practices involves much more than theoretical training or lectures. It requires:

• Deep, immersive engagement with the community

• Keen observation

• A passion-driven mindset

By fostering these practices through immersion, active observation, data collection, and emotional connection, teams can cultivate profound empathy, leading to more meaningful and impactful solutions.

The process isn't just about understanding the problem—it's about understanding the person behind it and designing from their perspective.

Tools and Methods for Understanding the Needs and Feelings of Customers or Stakeholders

Understanding customers' or stakeholders' needs and emotions is crucial for creating solutions that genuinely address their challenges. Various tools and methods can be used in this context, emphasizing design thinking and usability engineering. These techniques help uncover deep insights, allowing teams to connect with users practically and emotionally.

Journey Mapping: Visualizing Customer Experience

Journey mapping is a core tool used in design thinking to understand a customer's or stakeholder's experience. It involves mapping a user's journey when interacting with a product, service, or system.

• **Capturing Specific Events:** A journey map breaks down the process into specific events or touchpoints, from the first interaction to the outcome. This method helps teams identify pain points, frustrations, and positive experiences that a user might encounter.

For example, in a healthcare setting, the journey could start with scheduling an appointment and end with post-treatment follow-up, with every step mapped out in detail.

• **Understanding Emotions:** By observing and analyzing how customers feel at each journey stage, teams can gain insights into emotional triggers—

There are moments when a user may feel anxious, satisfied, confused, or frustrated. Understanding these emotions helps design solutions that meet functional needs and create a positive emotional experience for users.

• **Application of Neutralization:** Journey mapping also involves neutralization, where teams account for various biases that might arise from different user experiences.

For example, two users may interact with the same service differently based on their backgrounds, preferences, or environments.

Neutralization ensures that the insights gained reflect a more balanced view of user experiences.

While no single tool or method guarantees a complete understanding of customers or stakeholders, combining techniques like journey mapping, concept mapping, heat maps, prototyping, questionnaires, and role-playing can offer profound insights. By leveraging these tools, teams can gather quantitative and qualitative data, ensuring they understand what users need and how they feel and interact with the product or service. This holistic approach helps create functional and emotionally resonant solutions, leading to better outcomes for the team and its stakeholders.

Several tools and methods can be employed better to understand the needs and feelings of customers or stakeholders, blending human-centered design with empathy and data-driven techniques. Design thinking is one of the most widely used frameworks, emphasizing understanding the customer journey. Within this framework, tools like journey maps and concept maps help visualize customer interactions, allowing businesses to identify key pain points and areas of improvement. Prototyping is also crucial in collecting stakeholder feedback by simulating real-world experiences and refining products or services based on user input.

Observing behavioral patterns is essential in addition to these design tools. Techniques like heat maps track user interaction on websites or digital platforms, while surveys and questionnaires provide direct feedback on user experiences. These insights are further enriched by collaborative tools like brainstorming and role-playing, which encourage stakeholders to contribute creative solutions and empathize with user needs.

Empathy is at the heart of decision-making, reinforced through the Triple Bottom Line (TBL) approach. This method emphasizes financial performance, social impact, and environmental sustainability. Companies incorporating this approach make more informed, ethical decisions, balancing profit with societal and environmental responsibilities. This leads to sustainable growth that resonates with both customers and stakeholders.

Industries Where Empathy is Crucial

Empathy is vital in several industries, particularly those directly impacting human well-being. Some sectors where empathy plays an even more crucial role include:

1. Healthcare: Prioritizing Patient Needs Over Profit

Empathy is not just beneficial; it is essential in the healthcare industry. Healthcare providers must understand and prioritize patients' needs and feelings to deliver effective and compassionate care. This means looking beyond profitability to ensure services are accessible to all segments of society, including those who may not afford premium healthcare.

Aravind Eye Hospital's Cross-Subsidy Model: A prime example of empathy in action is Aravind Eye Hospital in India, which operates on a cross-subsidy model. Wealthier patients pay for treatment, allowing free or subsidized care for those who cannot afford it. This ensures high-quality care regardless of a patient's financial status and prioritizes accessibility over profit margins.

Understanding Diverse Patient Needs: Healthcare providers must consider patients' diverse backgrounds and scheduling needs.

For example, working professionals may require faster outpatient services that do not interfere with their work schedules. By creating specialized outpatient departments tailored to different demographics, healthcare institutions can enhance the patient experience while ensuring inclusivity.

2. Education: Fostering Inclusive Learning Environments

Empathy also plays a critical role in education, where understanding students' emotional and social needs is paramount. Educational institutions must create environments that foster learning while considering students' personal and socio-economic challenges.

• **Supporting Socio-Economic Barriers:** Many students struggle with financial difficulties, learning disabilities, or family obligations that impact their education. Schools and universities that offer scholarships, flexible learning schedules, and mentorship programs demonstrate empathy by addressing these challenges head-on.

• **Mental Health Support & Counseling:** Institutions implementing mentorship programs and counseling services demonstrate empathy by addressing students' emotional and mental health needs.

Schools and universities prioritizing well-being create an environment where students feel supported and motivated to succeed. For instance, peer mentorship programs help students navigate academic and personal challenges, fostering a sense of community and support.

3. Social Enterprises

Social enterprises aim to address societal challenges while generating revenue. Empathy is crucial for understanding the communities they serve and developing effective and respectful solutions to cultural and social dynamics. By directly engaging with these communities, social enterprises can tailor their offerings to meet the specific needs and aspirations of the individuals they aim to help.

Empathy is a soft skill and a strategic imperative that fosters sustainable practices and solutions resonating with diverse populations. Healthcare, education, and social enterprises benefit significantly from an empathetic approach. By prioritizing the needs and emotions of customers and stakeholders, these industries can promote inclusivity, enhance service delivery, and ultimately create a meaningful social impact.

Balancing Empathy with Tough Business Decisions

Balancing empathy with difficult business decisions is a complex challenge, particularly in sectors like healthcare and education. Here's a closer look at how leaders can navigate this balance:

1. Understanding the Dual Role

In the corporate world, leaders often wear two hats. One focuses on the operational side, prioritizing business metrics such as profitability, shareholder value, and quarterly performance. This approach sometimes requires making difficult, seemingly unemotional decisions, such as cost-cutting measures that may lead to layoffs.

Operational Focus:

• Prioritizes profitability and performance metrics (e.g., quarterly results).

• Involves tough decisions like cost-cutting and layoffs, which may seem transactional.

Conversely, the second hat represents the empathetic side of leadership, which emphasizes understanding the needs of employees, customers, and the community. This aspect is particularly relevant in Corporate Social Responsibility (CSR) initiatives, where businesses allocate a portion of their profits to projects that create a positive social impact, such as community service, healthcare programs, or environmental sustainability efforts.

Empathetic Focus:

• Emphasizes understanding and addressing the needs of employees, customers, and the broader community.

• Involves initiatives that foster a compassionate workplace culture and social impact.

2. Implementing Corporate Social Responsibility (CSR)

CSR serves as a bridge between operational efficiency and empathy-driven leadership. By establishing a structured CSR program, businesses can dedicate resources to initiatives that benefit the community while engaging employees in meaningful work beyond their daily responsibilities. For instance, employees may participate in local health drives, educational outreach programs, or environmental clean-up efforts during weekends. Such activities foster a culture of empathy within the organization while enabling companies to fulfill their social obligations.

Key Aspects of CSR Implementation:

• **Purpose of CSR:** Allocates a portion of profits to social impact projects (e.g., healthcare, education).

• **Employee Engagement:** Encourages participation in community service and outreach efforts.

Moreover, regulatory frameworks often mandate CSR spending, ensuring that funds allocated for social responsibility cannot be redirected for profit. This creates a clear boundary, enabling organizations to make meaningful contributions without the pressure of immediate financial returns.

Additional Benefits of CSR:

• **Regulatory Compliance:** Ensures CSR funds are used exclusively for social initiatives, preventing financial misallocation.

• **Cultural Impact:** Fosters a workplace culture of empathy, teamwork, and social awareness.

By integrating empathy into strategic decision-making and CSR efforts, businesses can balance profitability with a genuine commitment to social well-being, ultimately driving long-term success and positive societal impact.

3. Navigating Tough Decisions in Sensitive Sectors

Balancing empathy and business decisions becomes even more nuanced in sectors like healthcare and education. The stakes are higher, as decisions can directly impact people's lives. For instance, while a hospital may need to implement cost-saving measures, it is crucial to ensure that such decisions do not compromise the quality of patient care. This requires a deep understanding of the community's needs and the potential implications of any changes.

Sector-Specific Challenges

• Healthcare

o Maintaining the quality of care while implementing cost-saving measures is necessary.

o Decisions directly impact patients' lives, requiring careful consideration.

• Education: Budget cuts may affect teaching quality, necessitating stakeholder involvement.

• Human-Centric Approach

o Focus on Human Impact

o Consider how decisions affect employees, patients, and students.

o Engage with stakeholders to understand their needs and priorities.

4. Emphasizing the Human Aspect

A human-centric approach can guide leaders in making tough decisions. Leaders can navigate complex situations with empathy by focusing on the human impact of these decisions and considering how they affect employees, patients, or students. This may involve adopting a participatory approach, where stakeholders are actively involved in the decision-making process, ensuring their voices are heard and their needs addressed.

For example, budget cuts are necessary in education. Leaders might engage with teachers, parents, and students to understand their priorities and find ways to minimize the impact on educational quality. This approach builds trust and leads to more informed and compassionate decision-making.

Participatory Decision-Making

• Stakeholder Engagement

• Involve teachers, parents, and community members in discussions.

• Collect feedback to inform decisions and ensure inclusivity.

Trust Building

• Foster trust by demonstrating a commitment to understanding stakeholder perspectives.

• Create an environment where everyone feels valued and heard.

Balancing empathy with difficult business decisions requires a thoughtful approach that acknowledges the complexities of both roles. Leaders can effectively navigate this delicate balance by establishing clear CSR initiatives, focusing on the human aspect of decisions, and engaging stakeholders in the process. Ultimately, this approach supports the business's financial health while fostering a culture of empathy and social responsibility, contributing to long-term sustainability and success.

The Role of Empathy in Leadership

In today's rapidly evolving business landscape, leaders must increasingly wear two hats—one focused on hard metrics such as profitability and growth and another on the softer but equally essential aspects of empathy and social responsibility. Navigating this balance is both challenging and crucial for long-term success.

While corporate decisions often necessitate focusing on profits, frameworks like Corporate Social Responsibility (CSR) ensure businesses give back to society and maintain a human touch in their operations. These initiatives allow leaders to blend financial acumen with social impact, fostering a culture of inclusivity and care.

Developing Empathy in Leadership

Reflect on your interactions, both personal and professional. Do understanding and empathy guide them? Make a conscious effort to enhance your empathetic skills with the following steps:

• **Practice Active Listening** – Pay full attention to the speaker, understand their message, and respond thoughtfully.

• **Seek Feedback** – Regularly ask for and act on employee, customer, and peer feedback.

• **Cultivate an Inclusive Environment** – Encourage diverse perspectives and involve team members in decision-making.

• **Invest in Empathy Training** – Organize workshops or training programs to develop empathy among your team.

Empathy can bridge the gap between businesses and their stakeholders in an increasingly digital and impersonal world. Prioritizing empathy fosters meaningful connections, strengthens loyalty, and drives long-term success.

The Power of Empathetic Leadership

Empathetic leadership is about considering the human consequences of decisions, particularly in sectors where lives are directly impacted. Engaging with stakeholders, understanding their needs, and building trust are vital to making informed decisions that align with business goals and community well-being. This approach balances tough decision-making with compassion, ultimately driving sustainable growth by strengthening relationships with employees, customers, and society. Balancing empathy with complex decisions is not about choosing one over the other but integrating both to support business goals while nurturing a humane and socially responsible environment. This harmonious balance defines authentic leadership in today's world. Empathy is not just about feeling—it's about acting with compassion and understanding. As you progress in your business journey, remember that empathy can be your greatest asset. By integrating it into your core values and daily practices, you can transform your business and make a lasting impact on the world.

4

FROM COMPARISON TO PURPOSE

"Your purpose is not to be better than anyone else but to be better than you used to be."

— Unknown

C omparison is an integral part of human nature, and at some point, we all find ourselves trapped in the cycle of measuring our achievements against others. While many of us may try to avoid engaging in direct comparisons, society often pushes us into this mindset. This tendency becomes even more pronounced in the professional world, particularly in corporate environments, where appraisals, promotions, and recognition are often based on comparative metrics. Employees are evaluated against one another, creating an unhealthy cycle in which success feels valid only when it outshines others.

At some point in our lives, we have all fallen prey to the subtle yet destructive force of comparison. It is woven into the fabric of human nature—a reflexive response to gauge our standing by measuring ourselves against others. From childhood, we are conditioned to believe that our worth is tied to being better, faster, wiser, or more successful than the person next to us. Whether in school, at work, or even in our social lives, we cannot help but wonder: How do I stack up?

In today's world, the pressure to compare is relentless. We scroll through social media, witnessing glimpses of curated perfection, from career triumphs to picture-perfect vacations. Every achievement or milestone we reach is often met with an unspoken question: Am I doing enough compared to them? The trap lies in this cycle—an unending race that can leave us feeling hollow, even when we accomplish what we once longed for.

Nowhere is this comparison more insidious than in the professional world. In corporate environments, it becomes almost impossible to avoid. Appraisals, promotions, and success are frequently defined not by how well we have performed in our own right, but by how we measure up against our peers. We are ranked and categorized based on comparative metrics, subtly pitting us against another. While in the corporate trenches, I realized how deeply the comparison cycle had entangled my sense of achievement and self-worth. My wins felt validated only if they eclipsed someone else's. If I wasn't ahead, I wasn't truly succeeding.

But the comparison doesn't stop there—it follows us into every facet of life. It seeps into our personal goals, relationships, and even our self-perception. The constant pressure to measure up can erode our sense of purpose and leave us perpetually dissatisfied. It is a dangerous cycle, and escaping it requires a conscious shift in mindset. For me, that shift came during a pivotal moment in my career.

In the corporate environment, comparison is not just inevitable—it is institutionalized. Promotions, appraisals, and even day-to-day recognition are based on how well one performs relative to peers. This creates a culture where competition is celebrated, and success is validated only when it surpasses someone else's. Early in my career, I was caught in this rat race, tirelessly working to meet targets and exceed expectations—not for personal satisfaction, but simply to stay ahead. Yet, with each promotion and accolade, there was an unsettling hollowness. The rewards felt meaningless because a more profound sense of purpose did not drive them; they were merely the spoils of winning a competition I no longer wanted to participate in.

This wasn't a new experience for me. My first real encounter with the comparison cycle came long before I entered the corporate world. As a child, I was often measured against my classmates by well-meaning parents, teachers, and relatives. Like many children, I was pushed to excel academically, believing that competition would drive success. While some of my peers thrived in this environment, I found it troubling. I saw classmates relentlessly pursuing top grades and first-place finishes, often at the cost of their well-being. Some became discouraged, others disillusioned, and tragically, a few succumbed to the pressure in far more severe ways.

The comparison cycle followed me into adulthood, where the stakes were much higher. It was no longer about grades or trophies—now, it was about livelihoods, job satisfaction, and personal identity. The competition intensified, and the consequences became more serious. While I continued to advance in my corporate role, the constant pressure to outperform my colleagues wore me down. I longed for something more than just climbing the corporate ladder. I wanted a sense of purpose that transcended outshining others.

During this period of introspection, I reconnected with a childhood passion—electronics engineering. Growing up, while many of my friends competed for the top spots in class, I was immersed in radios, circuits, and gadgets, fascinated by how they worked. My sense of accomplishment back then wasn't driven by beating anyone else—it came from the joy of discovery and learning. That passion, buried under years of corporate competition, resurfaced as I grappled with the dissatisfaction of my work life.

Reflecting on my true interests and what genuinely brought me joy, I realized my ambitions didn't align with the corporate comparison game. I didn't want promotions or pay raises just to win them. I wanted to make a difference. This realization sparked a shift in my thinking, guiding me away from the relentless need to outshine others and toward a more meaningful path.

Leaving the corporate world was one of the most defining moments of my life. I shifted my focus to a field where my passion for electronics intersected with my desire to create a social impact: healthcare technology. I aimed to develop affordable, accessible medical devices to detect diseases like eye and kidney problems in rural areas. The work was deeply fulfilling, not because it allowed me to surpass anyone, but because it had the potential to make a real difference in people's lives. Success was no longer about comparison—it was about impact.

Of course, challenges didn't disappear. But they were different. The obstacles I faced weren't about competing with others; they were about solving real-world problems. The freedom I found in pursuing meaningful goals was liberating. No longer was I trapped in the exhausting comparison cycle, constantly measuring my worth against someone else's success. Instead, I set goals grounded in a deeper purpose, transcending external validation.

This journey taught me a vital lesson: comparison may be an inherent part of life, but it doesn't have to define us. When we become trapped in the comparison cycle, we lose sight of what truly matters—our personal growth, happiness, and the impact we can have on the world around us. Finding a purpose that aligns with our values and passions is the key to breaking free from comparison. For me, that purpose was healthcare technology. It may be entirely different for others, but the principle remains the same—when we set goals that genuinely matter to us, we liberate ourselves from the need to compare.

The more we feed into this comparative and competitive mindset, the more we lose sight of our true purpose. What starts as a seemingly harmless benchmark can slowly spiral into a constant feeling of being "less than." Our satisfaction becomes tethered to outperforming others, and we measure our happiness by someone else's standards. It's an exhausting way to live, leaving little room for genuine fulfillment.

Yet, breaking free from this cycle is far from easy. It requires a conscious decision to stop measuring our worth by external standards and instead embrace our unique journey. It's about shifting our focus away from what others are doing and toward discovering the deeper purpose that drives our lives. This is where fundamental transformation begins—we stop chasing someone else's definition of success and start living in alignment with what truly matters to us.

As we move through this chapter, we'll explore the subtle yet powerful ways comparison infiltrates our lives and how, by embracing purpose, we can finally free ourselves. When we live for our growth and fulfillment, we no longer need to compete for validation. The only comparison that genuinely matters is the one we make with ourselves.

The Individual Nature of Comparison

Comparison is an age-old concept that permeates various facets of human experience. It influences our decisions, self-worth, and mental health from childhood through adulthood. As we navigate the complexities of life, we inevitably find ourselves measuring our achievements against those of others. But can we break free from this cycle? Is there a universal approach to liberating ourselves from comparison, or is it a personal journey?

The answer lies in the nuanced understanding that comparison is not just an external phenomenon but also an internal struggle. While some may find solace in universally applicable strategies, the reality is that each individual's path to liberation from comparison is as unique as their experiences and values.

To understand why comparison is such a profoundly personal journey, we must first acknowledge the individualistic nature of our experiences. Each person carries a unique set of backgrounds, cultures, beliefs, and aspirations that shape their understanding of self-worth. While some may thrive on competition and seek validation through external achievements, others may prioritize introspection and personal growth.

For many, the realization that comparison serves little purpose often comes after years of struggle. This awakening is a turning point, prompting individuals to seek ways to disengage from the rat race of constant evaluation. Some find this through conversations with mentors or spiritual guides, while others look inward, discovering their passions and purpose. Ultimately, the journey is influenced by personal context—what works for one may not resonate with another.

The Intersection of Individuality and Commonality

While the journey to break free from comparison is deeply personal, it is also marked by common threads. Many people discover that their strategies for overcoming comparison often intersect. For instance, someone who begins by seeking guidance may later find that pursuing a hobby offers an outlet for their creativity. Similarly, individuals driven by a sense of purpose may find community and support through the shared experiences of others on similar journeys.

It's essential to recognize that although these paths can differ widely, they often share the same underlying goal: personal growth and liberation from the constraints of external evaluation. This shared objective fosters a sense of community among those on their journeys, providing opportunities for connection and support.

The Double-Edged Sword of Social Media

In the digital age, social media has transformed how we connect, share, and perceive our lives and the lives of others. While it offers a platform for creativity, community, and information, it also fosters a pervasive culture of comparison that can harm our self-worth.

Social media platforms often showcase curated highlights of people's lives—beautiful photos, extravagant vacations, and seemingly flawless achievements bombard our feeds daily. It is easy to compare our everyday reality with these idealized portrayals. Studies have shown that individuals who spend significant time on social media often develop a distorted view of their own lives.

This constant exposure to the "highlights" of others can lead to feelings of inadequacy, low self-esteem, and even depression.

For instance, someone scrolling through their Instagram feed may see a friend's luxurious holiday in Bali, followed by another acquaintance showcasing their recent promotion. In contrast, their routine may seem mundane, leading to a nagging sense of dissatisfaction. This social media-driven narrative fosters an unhealthy cycle of comparison, where individuals begin to believe that their self-worth is contingent upon how they stack up against others.

The Fake Facade

One of the most dangerous aspects of this culture of comparison is that many of the images and stories we see on social media are curated and often manipulated. People frequently edit their photos, highlight only the most glamorous aspects of their lives, and even fabricate experiences to garner likes and admiration. The rise of influencers and social media personalities exacerbates this issue, as their content often presents an unattainable standard of beauty, success, and lifestyle.

Take, for example, the phenomenon of weight loss advertisements that proliferate on social media. Promising drastic results with minimal effort, these ads prey on insecurities, presenting before-and-after photos that may not accurately reflect the individual's journey. For those struggling with body image or self-acceptance, such narratives can lead to unhealthy choices, including extreme dieting or excessive exercise, all in pursuit of an ideal that is often unrealistic and potentially harmful.

The Impact on Mental Health

The effects of this culture of comparison can be profound. As individuals continually measure their lives against the fabricated successes of others, they may find themselves in a downward spiral of negative self-talk and diminished self-worth. Research indicates that heavy social media users are more likely to experience symptoms of anxiety and depression, particularly among young adults and adolescents who are still forming their identities.

In extreme cases, this comparison culture can lead to tragic outcomes. Some individuals may become so overwhelmed by feelings of inadequacy that they see no way out, leading to severe mental health crises, including thoughts of self-harm or suicide. Social media can create an echo chamber where feelings of despair are magnified as individuals internalize the belief that everyone else is succeeding while they are failing.

The Positive Potential of Social Media

Despite social media's numerous pitfalls, it is essential to recognize its potential for positive impact. Social media can serve as a support, connection, and education platform. Individuals can share their stories, find communities that resonate with their experiences, and access a wealth of knowledge to help them navigate challenges.

For example, many people use social media to raise awareness about mental health issues, share their struggles, and provide a space for others to do the same. Open conversations can normalize discussions about mental health, providing solace to those who may feel isolated in their experiences. In this way, social media can foster a sense of community and belonging, countering the isolating effects of comparison.

Moreover, social media can be a powerful tool for education. With access to vast amounts of information, individuals can learn about topics that interest them, from cooking and photography to complex scientific concepts. Platforms like YouTube and Instagram host countless tutorials and educational content, making knowledge more accessible. This democratization of information empowers individuals to pursue their passions and develop new skills, promoting personal growth rather than comparison.

Handling the Comparison Trap

To harness the positive aspects of social media while mitigating its harmful effects, individuals must cultivate mindfulness and discernment in their social media usage. Here are several strategies to consider:

• **Limit Exposure** – Be intentional about the accounts you follow. Curate your feed to include content that uplifts, educates, and inspires rather than fosters comparison. Unfollow or mute accounts that trigger negative feelings or insecurities.

• **Engage Critically** – Approach the content you consume with a critical eye. Remember that social media often showcases a curated reality, not the whole picture. Recognize that everyone has struggles, even if they are not visible online.

• **Focus on Growth** – Shift your mindset from comparison to personal growth. Set individual goals and celebrate your achievements, no matter how small. Use social media as a platform to document your progress rather than compare yourself to others.

• **Limit Screen Time** – Be mindful of the time spent on social media. Set boundaries to prevent mindless scrolling and foster more meaningful offline interactions.

• **Cultivate Real Connections** – Seek out in-person relationships. Engage with friends and family without the filter of social media, fostering deeper connections that provide genuine support and understanding.

• **Practice Gratitude** – Regularly reflect on your achievements and what you are grateful for. This practice can help shift your focus from what you lack to what you have, fostering a sense of contentment.

As social media continues to shape our culture, it is crucial to navigate this landscape mindfully. The rise of social media has exacerbated the culture of comparison, significantly impacting self-worth and mental health. However, we can mitigate these adverse effects by cultivating critical content awareness and focusing on personal growth and authentic connections.

When used mindfully, social media can be a powerful inspiration, connection, and education tool. By embracing authenticity and recognizing our unique journeys, we can transform the culture of comparison into one of empowerment and support. Ultimately, the goal is not to measure ourselves against others but to appreciate our paths and celebrate the diverse experiences that make us who we are.

Navigating Moments of Relapse: How to Handle Resurfacing Feelings of Comparison

Comparison is an intrinsic part of life. No matter how much personal growth one experiences or how much one works toward self-awareness, the tendency to compare inevitably resurfaces.

Comparison is woven into the fabric of human existence, affecting us personally and professionally from childhood to adulthood. This cycle seems endless—from being compared to peers in school to facing performance reviews at work. So, how do we manage those moments of relapse when old feelings of inadequacy and comparison return?

The key lies not in avoiding these feelings altogether but in how we handle them. For me, managing these relapses has been a journey of self-reflection, purpose, and mental recalibration. From a young age, comparison is almost a rite of passage. In school, children are often measured against each other through grades, athletic performance, or extracurricular achievements. This conditioning continues through higher education and into professional life, where metrics like job performance, salary increases, promotions, and peer recognition keep the comparison cycle alive.

Recognizing that this tendency to compare is deeply embedded in societal structures is crucial. In many cases, comparison can serve as a motivator, pushing individuals to work harder or aim higher. However, the danger lies in letting it define one's sense of self-worth. There is a significant difference between using comparison as a tool for growth and allowing it to diminish one's value.

Keeping Your Bigger Objective in Sight

One of the most effective strategies I've learned for handling moments of relapse is to keep my more significant objective in focus. Whenever feelings of comparison arise, I ask myself, "What is my end goal?"

For example, in my professional life, I may be compared to others for promotions or salary hikes. Rather than dwelling on the immediate disappointment of not being promoted this year, I remind myself of the long-term objectives I'm working toward. Perhaps a promotion is delayed, but if I continue doing work that aligns with my greater purpose, the delay becomes less significant.

I've also learned from mentors that setbacks are temporary. You might not receive the recognition you hoped for today, but that doesn't mean it won't come tomorrow. A colleague once shared advice from his mentor: "Don't fixate on the failures. Keep doing good work, and the recognition will follow in time." This simple yet powerful insight has proven invaluable when comparison threatens to take over.

Focusing on Personal Growth, Not External Benchmarks

Another essential strategy is shifting the focus from external comparison to internal growth. When you constantly measure yourself against others, you risk becoming disconnected from your progress. Instead of asking, "Am I doing better than this person?" I've learned to ask, "Am I doing better than yesterday?"

This shift in perspective has been transformative for me. Rather than letting external benchmarks dictate my value, I evaluate my journey. For example, I reflect on how I performed last week or even last year, asking myself whether I've grown, learned, or improved in some way.

This simple shift allows me to break free from the comparison trap and stay grounded in my experience.

I've found this particularly helpful in areas where improvement is more subjective, such as health or personal development. For instance, I track my physical fitness with a smartwatch, not to compare myself with others but to monitor my progress. I will never compete with professional athletes, but that's not the point. The goal is to become better than I was yesterday, and that's enough to keep me motivated and focused.

The Role of Hobbies in Mental Recalibration

One of the most practical ways I've seen people manage stress and comparison is by engaging in hobbies. Some of my colleagues have found that participating in activities like photography, dancing, or sports gives them a sense of joy and accomplishment that isn't tied to professional success or comparison. These hobbies serve as a form of mental recalibration, offering a release from the pressures of day-to-day work and the inevitable comparisons that come with it.

I've seen this with a friend who participates in dance classes every weekend. For her, dancing isn't about being the best in the group—it's simply a way to decompress, focus on something she loves, and reconnect with herself. Similarly, others find hiking, painting, or cooking provides a creative outlet unrelated to external validation. Engaging in these activities helps shift the focus to personal joy and satisfaction rather than constantly measuring oneself against others.

I enjoy swimming as a way to reset and recalibrate. Although I started swimming later in life, at age 50, I don't compare myself to the younger swimmers around me. Instead, I track my progress using my smartwatch, focusing solely on how I'm improving over time. This approach keeps me motivated without the pressure of external comparison. On days when I forget to charge my watch, I find myself less motivated to swim, not because I'm comparing myself to others, but because I lose that personal feedback loop. This experience serves as a reminder that the most meaningful comparisons are the ones we make with ourselves.

Handling Relapse with Self-Compassion

Even with these strategies in place, moments of relapse are inevitable. Comparison, after all, is a deeply ingrained human trait.

In those moments, I've found that self-compassion is essential. Rather than criticizing myself for falling back into the comparison trap, I step back and acknowledge that these feelings are normal.

When comparison creeps in, I remind myself that I'm human. Everyone experiences these moments, even those who appear to have everything under control. By practicing self-compassion, I can release the guilt or frustration that often accompanies feelings of inadequacy and refocus on my journey.

I've also learned that relapses can be opportunities for reflection. Why am I feeling this way? What triggered these feelings of comparison? By asking these questions, I can often trace the source of my discomfort and address it directly. Sometimes, it's as simple as realizing I'm feeling overwhelmed or stressed, which gives me the clarity to step back and prioritize self-care.

Ultimately, while we may never completely escape comparison, we can learn to manage it in healthier, more constructive ways. By focusing on a larger purpose, shifting our attention to personal growth, engaging in meaningful hobbies, and practicing self-compassion, we can transform moments of relapse into opportunities for growth.

Comparison is not the enemy—how we react to it makes all the difference.

With the right mindset and tools, we can gracefully navigate these moments, using them as stepping stones on our journey toward self-discovery and fulfillment.

A Shift in Perspective

In high school, I had already begun questioning the value of comparison. Surrounded by peers laser-focused on becoming doctors, engineers, or securing top positions, I was drawn to electronics. I remember being captivated by radios and circuits, learning about diodes and transistors while my classmates pursued top grades. But even then, the pressure of comparison was always present. I wasn't immune to it, and while I wasn't always at the top of my class, the need to keep up with my peers lingered.

A turning point came during my internships and work at the Indian Institute of Science, where I saw the potential to combine my passion for electronics with healthcare. I worked on early projects involving medical devices, including a total blood cell counter, which showed me how electronics could impact healthcare. This intersection of engineering and medicine opened my eyes to the possibilities of making a difference without abandoning my passion.

Later, while working at a telecommunications company in Stockholm, I was exposed to even more opportunities to leverage technology for healthcare solutions. From remote monitoring systems for cardiac patients to projects using data services to monitor patients from home, I began to see how my skills could directly improve healthcare outcomes. This was when my focus shifted entirely—no longer motivated by competition, I was driven by the desire to create something meaningful.

After joining Philips and delving deeper into medical electronics, I worked on image-processing software and other diagnostic tools. Each project strengthened my belief that engineering could profoundly impact healthcare when applied with purpose. However, corporate constraints still limited my ability to make the broader impact I sought. I eventually realized that to align my work with my vision, I needed to step out and forge my path.

Finding Purpose: The Guiding Light

The cornerstone of avoiding comparison is discovering a personal sense of purpose. When I align my actions with a meaningful goal, I shift my focus from how I measure up against others to the progress I make within myself. A strong sense of purpose provides motivation and clarity, guiding me through challenges and steering me away from the distractions of external validation.

I recall a poignant story from my school days about a friend who struggled with comparison. Despite being below average in academics, he consistently measured his grades against those of his high-achieving classmates. Each exam left him feeling defeated, and he grappled with self-worth, believing that his academic performance defined his value.

One day, a compassionate teacher noticed his struggle and offered a simple yet profound advice: "Marks and grades never determine a person's ability to succeed; determination does." These words resonated deeply with him, transforming his mindset. Instead of comparing his success to others, he focused on his growth and pursuing his interests.

This shift allowed him to redefine success on his terms, ultimately leading to a more fulfilled life.

Embracing Individual Progress

A crucial aspect of moving away from comparison is measuring my progress against myself rather than others. As my friend learned, the key to personal growth lies in comparing today's efforts to yesterday's. This mindset fosters self-improvement, encouraging me to focus on my strengths and weaknesses while taking actionable steps toward growth.

One effective way to implement this practice is by setting specific, achievable goals. I create a unique roadmap tailored to my circumstances by defining what success looks like for me individually. For example, if physical fitness is my goal, rather than comparing myself to fitness influencers or elite athletes, I establish personal benchmarks, such as increasing the distance I can run or the number of push-ups I can perform. By tracking my progress and celebrating small victories, I cultivate a sense of accomplishment that boosts my confidence and drives me forward.

Additionally, incorporating a daily or weekly reflection practice helps reinforce this focus on individual progress. Journaling about what went well and what I can improve allows me to cultivate gratitude and self-awareness. This practice encourages me to acknowledge my efforts, no matter how small, and recognize my unique journey.

The Role of Mindset in the Journey

A common factor among those seeking to break free from comparison is the power of mindset. Developing a growth mindset—the belief that abilities and intelligence can be developed—can transform how individuals perceive their progress. This mindset encourages viewing challenges as opportunities for learning rather than benchmarks for comparison.

Adopting a growth mindset helps individuals appreciate their unique journey. Instead of fixating on what others have achieved, they can focus on their progress, however small. This shift in perspective fosters resilience and cultivates satisfaction in personal development.

Developing a growth mindset is essential in overcoming the tendency to compare. As psychologist Carol Dweck coined it, a growth mindset embodies the belief that abilities and intelligence can be developed through dedication, hard work, and persistence. Embracing this perspective shifts the focus from a fixed view of talent to an understanding that growth is a continuous process.

To cultivate a growth mindset, I must first recognize that challenges and failures are opportunities for learning rather than setbacks. When encountering difficulties, I ask myself, "What can I learn from this experience?" This reframing encourages resilience and fosters a sense of control over my personal development.

For instance, I remember my experience with swimming at fifty. Instead of comparing myself to younger swimmers, I embraced my journey by focusing on my improvement. I tracked my progress using a smartwatch, celebrating every stroke I swam and every second I improved. This commitment to personal growth kept me motivated, even when I faced setbacks.

Surrounding Myself with Supportive Influences

The people I surround myself with significantly shape my mindset and attitudes. To successfully avoid comparison, it is crucial to cultivate relationships with those who uplift and inspire me rather than those who foster competition and envy. Supportive friends and mentors provide encouragement, share their struggles, and remind me of my inherent worth.

Creating a network of individuals with similar values and goals amplifies my commitment to personal growth. Engaging with online or in-person communities that celebrate individuality and diversity, rather than conformity, provides platforms for sharing experiences, exchanging knowledge, and fostering a sense of belonging.

Additionally, I must set boundaries around my social media consumption and other comparison-inducing environments. By consciously choosing whom I follow and engage with, I can curate my online experiences to prioritize positivity and encouragement. Unfollowing accounts that trigger feelings of inadequacy creates a healthier space where I can focus on my journey.

Practicing Self-Compassion

In my pursuit of self-improvement, I recognize the importance of practicing self-compassion. The journey away from comparison can be challenging, and setbacks are inevitable. When I approach myself with kindness and understanding, I create a nurturing environment for growth.

Self-compassion involves treating myself with the same care and concern I would offer to a friend facing difficulties. Instead of berating myself for perceived failures or shortcomings, I acknowledge my humanity and the natural struggle of navigating personal challenges. Practicing self-compassion allows me to maintain motivation and resilience without succumbing to the pressures of comparison.

Engaging in mindfulness practices, such as meditation or deep breathing exercises, enhances my ability to cultivate self-compassion. These practices encourage me to remain present in the moment and develop a non-judgmental awareness of my thoughts and feelings. As I build this foundation of self-acceptance, I become better equipped to navigate the challenges of comparison.

Celebrating My Unique Journey

Ultimately, the journey away from comparison is about celebrating my unique path. I possess distinct talents, experiences, and perspectives that shape my life. Instead of viewing others as competition, I embrace a sense of community and collaboration, recognizing that we are all on individual journeys toward fulfillment.

One powerful practice is gratitude. Regularly reflecting on what I am thankful for shifts my focus from what I lack to what I have. By celebrating my achievements—big or small—I cultivate a mindset of abundance rather than scarcity. This perspective fosters contentment and allows me to appreciate my progress.

Additionally, embracing the belief that there is enough success for everyone alleviates feelings of jealousy or inadequacy. By cheering on others and celebrating their successes, I foster a sense of camaraderie that uplifts everyone involved. In doing so, I create a culture of support and encouragement that benefits us all.

Navigating away from comparison requires conscious effort and a commitment to personal growth. By focusing on purpose, measuring my progress against myself, cultivating a growth mindset, surrounding myself with supportive influences, practicing self-compassion, and celebrating my unique journey, I can break free from the comparison cycle and embrace a more fulfilling life.

Different Paths to Liberation

Seeking Guidance: For some, the journey begins by seeking guidance from mentors or spiritual leaders. Discussing self-worth, identity, and purpose can illuminate the path away from comparison.

These conversations often resemble personal counseling sessions, albeit with a spiritual twist. Whether reading self-help literature or attending workshops, gaining insight from those who have navigated similar struggles can be empowering.

Pursuing Passions: Another effective way to break free from comparison is by immersing oneself in hobbies or passions. Many individuals discover that engaging in photography, painting, dancing, or music is a conduit for self-expression. These pursuits allow them to shift their focus from external validation to internal satisfaction. Time spent on hobbies becomes a sanctuary, fostering creativity and personal fulfillment that is often missing in competitive environments.

Finding Purpose in Service: For others, liberation from comparison is found in pursuing a greater purpose—specifically, the desire to impact society positively. Many individuals channel their experiences, skills, and networks to create meaningful change. This pursuit may involve volunteering, starting community projects, or advocating for social causes. The focus shifts from individual accolades to collective impact, promoting a sense of belonging and contribution that supersedes the need for comparison.

Setting Personal Goals: Setting personal goals is crucial for breaking free from comparison. Individuals can establish goals tailored to their unique circumstances, aspirations, and values. This flexibility allows for diverse monetary, experiential, or spiritual achievements. The emphasis shifts from seeking external validation to prioritizing self-satisfaction.

Mindfulness and Acceptance: Incorporating mindfulness practices into daily life can help individuals avoid the compulsion to compare. Mindfulness encourages self-awareness and acceptance of one's current state, promoting peace and grounding. Through meditation or simple reflective practices, people learn to appreciate their journey without the constant pressure of comparison.

Cutting Off Comparison Through Purpose

In today's world, it's too easy to fall into the comparison trap. Social media, workplace environments, and relationships offer countless opportunities to measure ourselves against others. Whether it's comparing career paths, lifestyles, or successes and failures, this habit often leaves us feeling inadequate, frustrated, and lost.

But what if discovering your purpose is the key to breaking free from this cycle? Living with purpose creates a profound shift, turning your focus inward and helping you move beyond the superficial comparisons that often fuel insecurity and self-doubt. When you connect with your purpose, the external noise fades, allowing you to live a life shaped by your values and passions, not by someone else's standards.

How Comparison Steals Fulfillment

Comparison is a thief of joy. When you constantly measure your achievements, appearance, or life milestones against others, you drain your sense of self-worth. You may ask yourself, "Why am I not where they are?" or "Why don't I have what they have?"

The danger of comparison is that it shifts your attention away from your unique path and talents, forcing you to focus on someone else's journey. This distortion makes connecting with your true purpose harder, leaving you feeling unfulfilled and disconnected from what truly matters.

Purpose as the Antidote to Comparison

Purpose acts as a powerful antidote to comparison. When you're clear on your values and the unique reasons that drive you, the urge to compare yourself to others diminishes. Instead of seeking validation from external sources, you derive satisfaction from living in alignment with what matters most to you.

Discovering your purpose anchors you to your journey, providing a sense of fulfillment that doesn't rely on outperforming others. Here's how purpose helps cut off comparison:

1. Purpose Aligns You with Your Values

One of the main reasons people fall into the comparison trap is that they lose sight of what truly matters to them. Instead, they focus on external markers of success—what society, family, or friends deem valuable. However, when you discover your purpose, you shift from trying to meet others' expectations to living according to your values.

Purpose brings clarity. It helps you identify what is most meaningful in your life—family, creativity, service, or personal growth. When you align with these values, external comparisons lose their power because your internal compass guides you.

2. Purpose Creates Authentic Fulfillment

Many people chase goals because others praise them, whether it's a prestigious job, a higher income, or a particular lifestyle. However, these external benchmarks rarely lead to long-term satisfaction. Achieving them often fuels even more comparison, as the cycle never ends—there is always someone with more.

Purpose, on the other hand, brings authentic fulfillment. It's not about what you achieve relative to others but how well you align with what drives you. Every step you take feels meaningful when your goals are tied to your sense of purpose, regardless of how they compare to someone else's journey.

3. Purpose Redefines Success

Success is often measured by external factors—money, status, or popularity. When you constantly compare yourself to others, it's easy to fall into the trap of believing you're unsuccessful unless you have what they have. But purpose redefines success on your terms.

With purpose, success becomes a personal journey. It's about reaching milestones that matter to you—helping others, mastering a skill, or creating something meaningful. When you're living purposefully, you realize that success isn't a race against others but a fulfillment of your unique path.

4. Purpose: Builds Resilience

One of the hidden consequences of comparison is that it often leaves you feeling less than. Seeing someone else's success may make you feel inadequate, discouraging you from pursuing your goals. But when you're guided by purpose, you develop a more profound sense of resilience.

Purpose strengthens your connection to your inner self, making it easier to withstand life's ups and downs. When challenges arise, you're less likely to be discouraged by how others are doing and more focused on your progress. This resilience helps you stay the course, even when the temptation to compare yourself to others creeps in.

Breaking Free: Steps to Cut Off Comparison with Purpose

If you're struggling with comparison, here are some steps to help realign with your purpose and move away from the habit of measuring yourself against others:

a. Reflect on Your Core Values: Comparison often arises when we lose touch with what truly matters. Take time to reflect on your core values. What are the guiding principles in your life? When you align your actions with these values, comparison becomes irrelevant because you no longer live by someone else's standards.

b. Set Personal, Purpose-Driven Goals: Instead of setting goals based on what others are doing, define goals that align with your values and purpose. These goals should be meaningful to you, regardless of external recognition or validation. When your aspirations are tied to your purpose, you experience a deep sense of fulfillment that no comparison can diminish.

c. Practice Gratitude for Your Journey: Gratitude is a powerful tool to counteract comparison. Instead of focusing on what you lack, appreciate your unique journey. Celebrate your accomplishments and personal growth, no matter how small they may seem. Practicing gratitude shifts your focus from what others have to what you have achieved on your terms.

d. Surround Yourself with Purpose-Driven People: The company you keep can either fuel comparison or help you stay aligned with your purpose. Surround yourself with individuals who focus on their personal growth and purpose. These relationships inspire you to stay true to your path rather than encourage unhealthy comparisons.

e. Stay Curious and Embrace Growth: Comparison often stems from the fear of not measuring up. However, when you approach life with curiosity and a growth mindset, you remain open to learning and evolving. Purpose is not a fixed destination—it's a lifelong journey. Stay curious about your development and focus on your progress rather than how you compare to others.

Cutting off comparison is not about isolating yourself from the world or ignoring others' successes. It's about tuning out the noise and reconnecting with your inner values and purpose. When you are clear on your purpose, you no longer need to measure yourself against others because you live a life of meaning. You are no longer chasing someone else's dream but living your own.

Finding your purpose is the most powerful way to break free from the comparison cycle. It shifts your focus from external validation to internal fulfillment, allowing you to live with authenticity, joy, and success.

Breaking Free from Comparison: The Story of Innovation and Impact

The turning point in my journey came through an extraordinary project that challenged everything I had come to believe about success. During this time, I met Dr. Anand, a dedicated pediatric ophthalmologist, and began working on a mission to prevent blindness in preterm babies. This experience redefined my understanding of success and showed me how breaking free from the comparison cycle led to a more meaningful and fulfilling life.

The Corporate Comparison Trap

Before this project, my career was defined by comparison. The corporate environment fostered competition at every level, and success was always measured relative to others, by how well you performed compared to your peers. I chased one promotion after another, eager to prove my worth by surpassing others. Yet, despite climbing the corporate ladder, the expected sense of fulfillment never arrived. Each achievement only led to more comparison, competition, and a more profound sense of emptiness.

Looking back, it's clear that I had been measuring success by the wrong metrics. The external rewards—titles, bonuses, and praise—were fleeting, and my achievements felt hollow because they were driven by a desire to "win" rather than a genuine passion for my work. It was a cycle that seemed impossible to escape—until I found purpose beyond competition.

The Journey from Comparison to Purpose

As my team and I embarked on the journey to develop an affordable, portable device for ROP detection, the dynamics of my work completely changed. This wasn't about outperforming a competitor or gaining accolades. The stakes were different. Success in this project wasn't measured by how it compared to someone else's work; it was measured by the number of lives we could save.

But old habits die hard. Initially, I slipped back into familiar patterns, comparing our progress to other teams and existing products on the market. However, I soon realized that this was a dead end. Unlike the corporate world, where comparison was embedded in the structure of success, this project had no place for it.

There was no competitor to beat, no colleague to outshine. The only "competition" we faced was time—the sooner we developed a practical solution, the more babies we could save from preventable blindness.

As the project progressed, I experienced something new: the joy of working toward a purpose that transcended my ego. My engineering skills were being used not for recognition or accolades but to solve a problem that could change the lives of families across India. The sense of fulfillment I felt was far greater than any promotion or award I had received. For the first time, I wasn't looking at how my work compared to others—I was fully immersed in its purpose.

A Purpose-Driven Solution

The work wasn't easy. It took three years of research, prototyping, and refinement to develop a solution that met Dr. Anand's and my criteria. We needed a device small enough to fit on the back of a motorbike and affordable enough for widespread use in rural clinics. The original equipment was a massive, high-tech piece of machinery. However, we had to distill it to its most essential components, using cost-effective materials that could still deliver the same life-saving results.

The breakthrough came when we figured out how to create a portable device that was inexpensive and simple enough for a technician to operate in the field. Using telemedicine, these technicians could capture images of a baby's retina and send them to specialists like Dr. Anand, who would then remotely diagnose the condition. This system allowed us to reach babies in even the most isolated villages and screen them within the critical six-week window, enabling timely treatment before it was too late.

The results were transformative. As we deployed the device in rural areas, babies who would have otherwise lost sight received treatment in time. Families who had once believed blindness was inevitable were given newfound hope. It was a powerful reminder that real success doesn't come from comparison but from the impact we make on the lives of others.

A Shift in Focus: A Mission to Save Sight

My encounter with Dr. Anand began a profound shift in my perspective. Dr. Anand had spent years working to combat Retinopathy of Prematurity (ROP), a condition that causes preventable blindness in preterm babies. He explained that the primary barrier to saving these babies' sight wasn't a lack of medical knowledge but the inaccessibility of affordable, portable screening devices in rural India.

At the time, pediatric ophthalmologists relied on large, expensive equipment to diagnose ROP. While these machines were highly effective, their size, complexity, and cost—over $130,000 each—meant they were only available in major hospitals, far from the rural areas where most at-risk babies were born. The result was tragic: thousands of babies lost their vision each year, not because their condition was untreatable but because they couldn't be diagnosed in time.

The more Dr. Anand shared, the more I realized this was precisely the challenge I had been searching for—one that wasn't about competition or comparison but about making a tangible difference. It wasn't about outperforming anyone or rising above others, but solving a real-world problem that could transform lives.

The Influence of Mentors

Dr. Venkata Swami: A Visionary in Eradicating Blindness

Dr. Venkata Swami, the founder of Aravind Eye Care System, popularly know as Dr.V, has profoundly influenced my journey. His life's work revolved around eradicating avoidable blindness, and his vision was revolutionary. In a world where eye care is often overlooked, Dr. V recognized the urgent need to address the barriers preventing individuals from receiving basic eye care.

His approach extended beyond merely treating patients; he sought to understand the systemic issues contributing to the lack of access to healthcare. He conducted meticulous research to uncover why many people hesitated to seek medical attention. His efforts resulted in an eye hospital and a comprehensive eye care model that included outreach programs, community education, and innovative financing solutions. By offering affordable services and advocating for government reimbursement, Dr. V transformed eye care in India and inspired countless others to follow in his footsteps.

Dr. V relentless pursuit of his mission taught me the importance of having a clear purpose. His ability to drive meaningful change even after retirement was a powerful reminder that age is never a barrier to making a difference. His story inspired me to reflect on how I could contribute to my community, regardless of my background or resources.

The Ripple Effect of Passionate Individuals

Beyond Dr. V, my journey has been enriched by observing other remarkable individuals dedicated to various causes. I have encountered people committed to improving education, reforesting arid regions, and ensuring access to clean drinking water. Each mentor demonstrated how one person's commitment could ignite community-wide transformations.

For instance, I've witnessed individuals working tirelessly to plant trees in nearly desert-like conditions. They weren't just planting saplings but nurturing a vision of sustainability and environmental resilience. Their efforts improved local ecosystems and transformed the lives of individuals who depended on these resources. Witnessing their dedication reinforced my belief that meaningful change is always achievable when driven by purpose.

Similarly, I've encountered countless stories of individuals identifying the urgent need for clean water in their communities. Working with local governments and organizations turned an insurmountable challenge into a tangible reality. Their resilience inspired me to approach my endeavors with the same problem-solving mindset, no matter how daunting the obstacles initially appeared.

The Power of Literature

In addition to the influence of these remarkable individuals, literature has played a significant role in shaping my perspective. Books serve as influential teachers, offering insights, wisdom, and motivation that often linger long after turning the last page.

Books That Resonate

One book that profoundly impacted my thinking is The 7 Habits of Highly Effective People by Stephen R. Covey. Covey's framework emphasizes the importance of character ethics and personal accountability—principles that resonated deeply with me as I navigated my journey. His insights encouraged me to cultivate habits aligned with my values and prioritize tasks contributing to my long-term goals.

Another influential book is Man's Search for Meaning by Viktor E. Frankl. This powerful memoir details Frankl's experiences as a Holocaust survivor and his exploration of the human search for purpose. His assertion that meaning can be found even in the most harrowing circumstances struck a chord with me. It reinforced the idea that my journey, no matter how challenging, presents an opportunity for growth and self-discovery.

Inspiration from Biographies

Beyond self-help books, biographies of influential figures have also shaped my perspective. The life stories of Swamy Vivekananda, Nelson Mandela and Mahatma Gandhi highlight the extraordinary potential of human determination and resilience. Their journeys remind us that personal sacrifice and unwavering commitment to a cause can inspire movements and create lasting change. Studying their lives allowed me to draw parallels to my own experiences. Their lessons on perseverance encouraged me to remain steadfast in my pursuits, no matter the obstacles I faced. Each biography served as a potent reminder that hope can be a guiding light even in the darkest times.

Embracing the Journey

Reflecting on the influences that have shaped my transition, I am reminded of the importance of gratitude. I am deeply thankful for the mentors who have guided me, the books that have ignited my curiosity, and the individuals whose passions have sparked a fire within me. These experiences have collectively fostered a sense of purpose that propels me forward. I have realized that I am not just a passive observer in my life but an active participant in shaping my narrative. Inspired by my mentors, I strive to embody the principles of compassion and service, aiming to make a meaningful impact on my community.

As I continue my journey, I understand that this transition is ongoing. Life will always present challenges and opportunities for growth. However, I now possess the tools and perspectives to navigate these moments with confidence and resilience.

I remain committed to seeking out new mentors and engaging with inspiring literature. Every conversation with a mentor and every book page presents an opportunity to expand my understanding and refine my purpose. I recognize that the path to self-discovery is not solitary—the wisdom and experiences of others enrich it. The mentors and books that have guided me through this transition are not merely points of influence; they are integral threads woven into the fabric of my life. They have taught me the importance of purpose, resilience, and the power of community.

As I continue to learn and grow, I aspire to pass these lessons on to others, becoming a mentor in my own right. In a world filled with challenges, the legacies of those who have come before us remind us that change is possible. Through mentorship or literature, we can all find inspiration to navigate our journeys, overcome the barriers of comparison, and embrace the unique paths we are meant to follow. So, is there a universal approach to breaking free from comparison? The answer is nuanced. While specific themes and strategies may resonate across individuals, the journey is inherently personal. Each person must navigate their path, guided by their unique experiences, values, and aspirations.

The challenge lies in embracing our individuality while acknowledging our common everyday goals. In a world that constantly encourages comparison through social media, workplace competition, and societal expectations, it is essential to cultivate a mindset that prioritizes self-acceptance and growth.

Breaking free from comparison is not a one-size-fits-all endeavor. It is a deeply personal journey that invites introspection, exploration, and the discovery of one's true purpose. While universal themes may emerge, each person's path will be shaped by their experiences and goals.

As we navigate this intricate landscape, let us remember that the goal is not merely to escape comparison but to cultivate a deeper understanding of ourselves. By embracing our individuality and celebrating our unique journeys, we can create a life filled with fulfillment and meaning, free from the constraints of comparison.

Ultimately, success is not about being the best—it's about being the most impactful.

5

ALIGNING PASSION WITH PROFESSION

"The things you are passionate about are not random; they are your
calling."

— Fabienne Fredrickson

H ave you ever experienced the all-too-familiar Sunday evening
dread, knowing that Monday is just around the corner, signaling
the start of another workweek? Many people share this feeling of
impending monotony or stress as they prepare to return to a job that
may not ignite their enthusiasm.

But what would it take for you to wake up excited for the week ahead on
Monday morning?

A career that excites you—where your work feels purposeful and
fulfilling—can transform how you experience the workweek and
life. Instead of dreading Monday mornings, you eagerly anticipate
them because you're in a profession that fuels your passion. This
transformation is not just a dream; it is a tangible reality many have
achieved—and you can, too.

Many choose careers based on practicality, financial security, or societal expectations. While these factors are essential, the truth is that aligning your profession with your passion can unlock a level of job satisfaction and motivation that is hard to match. When you're passionate about what you do, work becomes more than just a paycheck—it becomes a source of inspiration and joy. Your tasks no longer feel like obligations; they become opportunities to engage in something that energizes you and aligns with your deeper values.

Realizing that passion and profession should be aligned is not always immediate or straightforward. It often comes after years of working in an environment where the two are misaligned or after witnessing someone successfully merge their passion with their career. Over the years, I've met countless individuals who struggled to balance what excites them and sustains them financially. But I've also seen others who found a way to merge the two, creating fulfilling and impactful careers.

From an early point in my career, I recognized that passion is essential for maintaining enthusiasm and energy. It fuels us through the mundane and the challenging. But the real challenge is translating that passion into a career that emotionally and financially sustains you.

To align your career with your passion, you must first understand what drives you.

How to Identify and Define Personal Passions

Identifying your passion is often presented as a simple task. We frequently hear the advice to "follow your passion"—especially at the start of our professional journey. The idea is compelling: find what excites you, and you'll naturally excel in your work. However, discovering and defining your true passion is far more intricate and personal. It's rarely a singular, straightforward realization; instead, it's an ongoing, sometimes lifelong process of introspection, experimentation, and refinement.

When I graduated as an engineer, I was bombarded with advice about following my passion, but no one told me how to find it. The challenge wasn't just identifying what excited me and understanding how my interests could translate into a meaningful career. I quickly realized that passion is not static; it evolves with time, circumstances, and new experiences. However, a few guiding principles helped me identify what truly fuels me.

Passion is not something you discover once and follow for the rest of your life. It is a constantly evolving process shaped by new experiences, discoveries, and personal growth. What excites you today may differ ten or twenty years from now. The key is to remain open to change, keep exploring, and allow your passion to evolve. Whether it becomes the foundation of your profession or remains a cherished hobby, passion enhances both the quality of your work and your overall fulfillment.

Once you've begun the journey of self-discovery, there are practical steps to align your passion with your career.

Ways to Identify and Align with Your True Passion

1. Self-Reflection and Paying Attention to Interests

Discovering your passion is, first and foremost, an inward journey. It requires deliberate self-reflection and a keen awareness of what energizes and motivates you. Passion is often hidden in the activities you look forward to, the tasks that make you want to jump out of bed in the morning.

This process began during my engineering studies. While many of my peers were drawn to the theoretical aspects of engineering, I found myself fascinated by hands-on work—creating and building things from scratch. My real passion started emerging when I first interacted with a new piece of technology: microprocessors.

It was the 1980s, and personal computers were not yet widely available. The machines we worked with in engineering schools were massive, expensive, and institutional. However, I was captivated by the potential of microprocessors—tiny yet powerful components capable of processing information faster than we had imagined.

That fascination led me to dive deep into the world of microprocessors, and soon, I was experimenting with building computer systems on my own. I would lose track of time, spending long hours assembling hardware and developing code to make it function. This experience helped me realize something profound:

The work that makes you lose track of time, that excites you beyond obligation—that is often where your passion lies.

Through self-reflection and exploration, I recognized that my love for technology, innovation, and problem-solving was not just an academic interest but something that truly energized me. That realization became the first step toward aligning my profession with my passion.

2. Experimentation and Testing the Waters

Identifying passion is not just about thinking or reflecting—it's about taking action and testing the waters. What fascinates us from a distance may not hold our interest when we engage with it more deeply. We might become infatuated with an idea, believing it to be our calling, but we can't know if it's a fleeting curiosity or a lasting passion until we put in the time and effort to explore it.

In my younger years, I was drawn to many things, including sports. I remember being mesmerized by pole vaulting when I saw a firdos effortlessly scale six-foot barriers using a bamboo pole. It looked exhilarating, and I convinced myself I wanted to pursue it. However, I quickly realized the risks and physical demands involved once I tried it. My enthusiasm faded, and I understood that not every initial interest becomes a lifelong passion. Some things captivate us from a distance, but they may not be the right fit for active participation.

The same realization came with other pursuits, such as photography and music. I found both fascinating, but as I invested time learning the craft, I realized they were better suited as hobbies than professional aspirations. Through these experiences, I learned that true passion is more than excitement—it's about what you're willing to dedicate time, effort, and even sacrifices to master. It's what challenges you to push through difficulties without losing enthusiasm.

3. The Role of Talent in Passion

Another critical lesson I learned is that passion and talent are not the same. You can have a deep passion for something, but that doesn't necessarily mean you have the natural talent to excel professionally. Many people love music—listening, analyzing, and discussing it—but not everyone can perform or compose.

The intersection of talent and passion became more evident as I delved deeper into engineering and technology. My talent for problem-solving and understanding complex systems complemented my passion for creating and innovating with technology. That synergy made it possible to turn my passion into a sustainable profession.

If you are passionate about something but lack the talent, you can still engage with it as a hobby or personal interest. However, aligning passion and talent creates the foundation for a fulfilling and successful career. The key is recognizing where your passion meets your strengths and focusing on that intersection to maximize enjoyment and success.

4. Passion vs. Profession

Once you enter the professional world, the stakes change. You are no longer just pursuing what excites you—you also have to earn a living and meet responsibilities. The ideal scenario is to find a profession that aligns with your passion, but this is not always possible. Many people work in careers that don't perfectly match their passions, and that's okay.

The key is identifying aspects of your passion within your profession, even if the two aren't entirely aligned. In my case, I eventually transitioned from academia to industry because I wanted to see my passion for technology come to life in a commercial setting. While I loved teaching, I realized that working in industry would provide the resources and environment necessary to explore product development, something I was deeply passionate about. However, even then, I had to balance the demands of my job with my creative aspirations.

Many professionals feel disillusioned when their work doesn't fully reflect their passion. However, every job offers different opportunities to infuse your passion into your work. For instance, a software engineer who loves music might not work in the music industry, but they can apply their creativity and discipline from music to coding.

Passion doesn't always have to translate directly into your daily tasks. Instead, it serves as a guiding force, shaping how you approach challenges, innovate, and find fulfillment in your work. Integrating passion into your professional mindset creates a meaningful and rewarding career, even if it's not a perfect match.

Instead of abandoning his passion for medicine, Dr. Venkataswamy redirected it toward a different yet equally impactful field—ophthalmology. Despite the physical limitations imposed by his arthritis, he trained himself to perform delicate eye surgeries with remarkable precision. His unwavering determination and resilience enabled him to master a profession that demanded steady hands and intricate skills, proving that passion can overcome even the most daunting obstacles.

Dr. Venkataswamy's contributions to ophthalmology extended far beyond individual patient care. He founded Aravind Eye Hospital, a pioneering institution dedicated to providing high-quality, affordable eye care to millions, particularly in underserved communities. Under his leadership, Aravind developed a self-sustaining model that provided free or low-cost treatment to those in need while ensuring financial viability through paying patients. His hospital has since become one of the world's most extensive eye care facilities, treating millions of people and restoring sight to countless individuals who would have otherwise remained blind.

His story is a testament to how aligning passion with profession can lead to transformative outcomes for oneself and society. Despite life's setbacks, his commitment to service and unwavering belief in making healthcare accessible turned his challenges into a global movement that continues to impact lives today.

Even with passion, the road isn't always smooth. This is where resilience becomes vital.

The Role of Resilience in Pursuing Passion

Dr. Venkataswamy's journey underscores an essential lesson: passion alone is insufficient. It must be accompanied by resilience, adaptability, and a willingness to redefine one's path in the face of obstacles. Many people believe that passion follows a straight line—that once they find it, success will come naturally. However, stories like his prove that adversity, redirections, and unexpected challenges often test passion.

Even those who achieve great success rarely do so without hardship, failures, and moments of doubt. What separates them from the rest is their ability to pivot, adjust their trajectory, and remain committed to the broader purpose behind their passion. Those who genuinely make an impact refuse to let setbacks define them, whether in art, science, business, or medicine.

Throughout history, individuals who aligned passion with purpose have left a lasting impact. Their journeys offer invaluable lessons.

Lessons from Passion-Driven Careers

From Da Vinci's insatiable curiosity to Franklin's relentless pursuit of knowledge and Dr. Venkataswamy's resilience in hardship, each figure exemplifies how passion and determination can lead to extraordinary achievements. Their stories highlight several critical lessons:

• Passion is dynamic. It evolves and is shaped by experiences, challenges, and self-discovery.

• Adversity does not mean the end of passion. Sometimes, the most significant setbacks become the stepping stones to a greater purpose.

• True fulfillment comes from aligning passion with impact. Whether through innovation, service, or creativity, the most rewarding careers are those that contribute to something beyond oneself.

• Success is not a linear journey. Every outstanding achievement involves trial, failure, and perseverance, but the ability to adapt ultimately leads to breakthroughs.

These examples inspire us to rethink how we define career success and fulfillment. Instead of searching for the "perfect job" or expecting passion to emerge instantly, we should approach our journeys with curiosity, adaptability, and a willingness to refine our interests over time. Doing so opens the door to careers that sustain us financially and enrich our lives with meaning and purpose.

I vividly remember spending countless late nights in the lab, poring over circuit diagrams, writing lines of assembly code, and troubleshooting issues that seemed impossible to solve. Each breakthrough, no matter how small, fueled my determination. It wasn't just about building a machine—it was about pushing the boundaries of what was possible and seeing my ideas take shape in the real world.

This hands-on experience was a turning point in my career. While many of my peers prepared for traditional corporate jobs, I became deeply engrossed in innovation and practical problem-solving. During this time, I realized something crucial: true passion is not just about interest but persistence. It's about spending long hours perfecting something simply because it excites you, not because someone expects it of you.

When passion becomes more than a hobby, it transforms into a profession.

Turning Passion into a Profession

Upon graduation, I faced a critical decision: Should I take the safe route and secure a stable job at a large firm or pursue my passion for computers and innovation, even if it meant uncertainty? The traditional path was tempting, but I knew deep down that I wanted to build something of my own—to create, innovate, and explore.

I chose the latter, and though the journey was anything but easy, it reinforced my belief that passion must be accompanied by courage and resilience. I went on to work with cutting-edge technology, exploring ways to make computing more accessible and solving real-world challenges in engineering, medical technology, and business. Looking back, following my passion was one of the best decisions of my life.

However, passion alone isn't always enough—it must align with opportunity.

The Intersection of Passion and Opportunity

One of the greatest lessons I've learned is that passion alone is not enough—it must meet opportunity at the right moment. Many people struggle to find this intersection, believing they must either pursue passion at the cost of financial stability or sacrifice passion for a practical career. But the truth is, the most successful professionals find ways to align their passion with real-world opportunities.

In my case, my passion for technology evolved as the industry itself grew.

The increasing demand for computing power, the expansion of medical electronics, and the rise of digital solutions all presented opportunities to apply my passion in impactful ways. I wasn't just working with technology for the sake of it—I was using it to solve problems, improve efficiency, and create meaningful innovations. That's the true power of aligning passion with profession—it leads to fulfilling and impactful work.

Lessons from a Passion-Driven Career

Reflecting on my journey, I've realized a few key takeaways about pursuing passion in one's career:

• Passion is discovered through action, not contemplation. Many people spend years searching for their passion when, in reality, passion often emerges through hands-on experience and experimentation. Try different things, dive into projects, and notice what excites you the most.

• Challenges are not obstacles—they are fuel. When you're passionate about something, the difficulties don't discourage you. Instead, they motivate you to push further. The long nights spent solving complex problems in my early years never felt like a burden; they were part of the thrill.

• Passion should be adaptable. It's not always about following a rigid dream—it's about adapting your passion to evolving interests and opportunities. Dr. Venkataswamy's story is a prime example; when his original path was no longer viable, he adapted, found a new way to pursue his deeper mission, and ultimately created an even more significant impact.

• Passion meets success when it solves real-world problems. Passion for its own sake is fulfilling, but becomes unstoppable when it aligns with a real need or challenge. This is where innovation happens—when passionate individuals find ways to apply their enthusiasm to meaningful problems.

• The most fulfilling careers are built on intrinsic motivation. When your work excites you and challenges you in the best way, you don't just succeed—you thrive. You wake up looking forward to the day because you're engaged in something that matters to you personally.

• Pursuing passion is not a single event; it's an ongoing journey of discovery and adaptation. Whether you're a student, an early-career professional, or an experienced leader, the key is to remain curious, open to new experiences, and willing to challenge yourself.

In a world where many people settle for careers that don't inspire them, those who find ways to align their work with their passion stand out—not only because they are more fulfilled, but because their enthusiasm drives them to achieve more, innovate better, and inspire others along the way.

I quickly realized that while my academic background had given me a strong foundation in engineering principles, the industry demanded different problem-solving that required practicality, efficiency, and an understanding of real-world applications. Unlike academia, where exploration was often theoretical, the industry required me to focus on delivering results, meeting deadlines, and ensuring that innovations could be scaled for impact.

As I transitioned into product development, I discovered that my passion wasn't just about technology but about using it to solve meaningful problems. My work now directly affects people's lives, whether developing medical electronics, improving communication systems, or designing hardware that enhances efficiency in various industries. This shift in focus—from theory to impact—became a defining moment in my professional journey.

One of the biggest challenges in aligning passion with profession is recognizing that the perfect opportunity doesn't always exist outright—sometimes, it must be created. While my passion for technology was always evident, finding the right avenue to channel it productively took me time.

Initially, I struggled with the constraints of working within an organization. Budgets, deadlines, and corporate priorities sometimes stifle creativity. However, I soon realized that within these constraints lay opportunities to innovate. If I balance my creative aspirations with business needs, I can make meaningful contributions while staying true to my passion.

I also learned that passion must be tempered with patience and adaptability. The real world doesn't always provide an immediate path to do what you love. Many professionals feel discouraged when their first job or project doesn't fully align with their passion. But as my journey showed, passion evolves when paired with experience, and sometimes, it takes time to find the perfect intersection of what excites you and sustains you.

Another revelation from my industry experience was the importance of collaboration. Unlike in academia, where individual research often drives progress, teamwork is the foundation of innovation in the industry. I learned to work alongside designers, developers, business strategists, and engineers, bringing different perspectives.

This collaborative approach helped refine my ideas, ensuring they were technologically sound but also practical, scalable, and market-ready. Passion alone can drive invention, but real-world impact requires collaboration, execution, and strategic thinking.

By working with teams, I expanded my vision beyond engineering and began to see technology as a tool for broader transformation, whether in healthcare, finance, communication, or social impact. It was no longer just about building great products but ensuring they served a meaningful purpose.

Looking back, my initial passion for technology was only a starting point. What truly drove me forward was the ability to create something that mattered—something that solved a real-world challenge and improved people's lives.

The lesson I carry forward is this: Passion is not static. It evolves, deepens, and finds new meaning when paired with experience, challenges, and real-world application. By moving beyond theoretical discussions and immersing myself in hands-on problem-solving, I was able to turn passion into purpose.

For anyone struggling to align their passion with their profession, the key is to remain curious, adaptable, and willing to take risks. Sometimes, the ideal career path isn't immediately visible. Still, you can carve out a fulfilling and impactful journey by exploring different environments, building skills, and staying committed to what excites you.

Of course, the journey wasn't without its challenges. One of the biggest obstacles I encountered was the perception of specific roles within the industry. Many young engineers I met were frustrated with what they saw as "boring" or "monotonous" jobs.

For instance, those in maintenance or testing roles often felt their work was uninspiring because it involved fixing existing systems rather than creating something new.

However, I found that these roles offered incredible opportunities for growth and learning. Working in maintenance, for example, requires a deep understanding of systems—how they work, where they fail, and how they can be improved. It is a job that forces you to think critically about design and function, and in doing so, it can ignite new passions for innovation and problem-solving. I have seen many young engineers transform their outlook on their careers after realizing that these so-called "boring" roles were providing them with invaluable experience and insights that could fuel their passion for creating better designs in the future.

Passion does not always have to mean inventing the next groundbreaking technology or starting a business from scratch. It can be about finding ways to innovate within the systems you already work in by improving existing products, optimizing processes, or contributing new ideas to a project. Over time, as you gain more experience and understand the nuances of your profession, you will find ways to bring your passion into your work, even in unexpected places.

Along the way, I have learned that passion and profession do not always align perfectly initially. Still, with experience, perseverance, and an open mind, you can find ways to bring the two together.

Ultimately, pursuing your passion is not just about personal satisfaction—it is about creating a professional life that allows you to make meaningful contributions to the world around you. Whether through teaching, industry, or entrepreneurship, the key is to stay connected to what drives you and find ways to incorporate that passion into your work. In doing so, you not only change your own life but also have the potential to impact the lives of others.

I have often had young professionals approach me, seeking advice on what they should do after completing their degrees, whether in engineering, medicine, or accounting. They usually have strong academic credentials and some interest in their field, but feel disconnected. They seek a way to align their passion with their profession, but often struggle to define that passion.

One such conversation stands out vividly. A close friend had completed his medical degree but found himself more drawn to management than practicing medicine. He did not want to specialize in a medical discipline; instead, he was fascinated by organizing and managing health systems. It was a difficult realization for him—he had invested years in medical school but was not passionate about becoming a specialist.

When he came to me, we discussed how he could align his newfound passion for management with his medical background. Eventually, we found an avenue through public health. He enrolled in a master's program in public health and discovered a world where he could merge his medical knowledge with his passion for organization, management, and improving health systems.

By pursuing public health, he did not have to abandon his medical background. Instead, he was able to apply his knowledge in a way that was meaningful to him and beneficial to society. He now manages healthcare systems, helping to optimize hospital operations and make healthcare more accessible and affordable.

His passion for management has been fully integrated into his profession, and as a result, he has thrived professionally and personally.

He is one of the busiest and most successful individuals I know today. His work spans multiple disciplines, from healthcare IT to policy forums, allowing him to contribute meaningfully to society. His journey illustrates the power of aligning passion with profession—when your job is not just a means to earn a paycheck but an extension of what excites and motivates you.

Not everyone can seamlessly align their passion with their profession. Many people pursue a particular path because it seems safe or practical, only to realize later that their true passion lies elsewhere. For instance, I have met numerous individuals passionate about music who end up in corporate jobs that leave little time to explore their musical interests. They face a difficult choice—should they continue in a stable profession, or take the risk of pursuing their passion full-time?

This is where the challenge lies. Blending a passion like music or photography with a demanding corporate job is difficult for most people. The pressures of meeting deadlines, managing projects, or overseeing production can leave little room for personal interests. While integrating hobbies into daily life—whether by using music as a stress reliever or joining a photography club—is possible, making those passions a central part of one's professional life is often not feasible.

The Dilemma of an Unaligned Passion and Profession

After years of working in fields like engineering or medicine, I have met people who realized their true passion was something entirely different—whether music, writing, or even automotive work. Some boldly decided to give up their stable professions and pursue their passion full-time, but this was a rare and risky move. Most people do not have the luxury of shifting gears after establishing a career.

The journey to aligning passion with profession is neither easy nor always straightforward. It requires self-reflection, experimentation, and sometimes a willingness to take risks. However, the rewards are immense when that alignment is found, bringing personal satisfaction and professional success.

For many, entrepreneurship is the most effective way to merge passion with profession. Starting a business allows you to design your career around what you love. Whether your passion lies in technology, healthcare, or the arts, entrepreneurship enables you to shape your work in a way that excites you.

Entrepreneurship offers a unique opportunity to integrate passion with profession. When you build something from the ground up, you can ensure it reflects your values, interests, and aspirations. Your business manifests your passion, making the work feel less like a burden and more like a natural extension of who you are and what you love.

Looking back on my career and the experiences of those around me, I have realized that when passion and profession are aligned, work becomes more than just a job. It becomes a means of self-expression, a way to contribute to society, and an opportunity to create something meaningful. Whether through entrepreneurship or by finding ways to integrate passion into an existing career, the key is to recognize the importance of this alignment and pursue it with intention and dedication.

When passion and profession become one, you unlock an infinite energy source. The lines between work and play blur, and you are driven by a desire to create, innovate, and make a difference. Financial rewards become secondary because the work itself is what truly fulfills you.

Why Is It So Hard to Turn Our Passions into a Profession?

Turning your passions into a profession may seem like an unattainable dream for many. Most people believe it is too late to change career paths, while others feel financially or personally constrained from making such a shift. But is that the real reason it is so difficult to turn our passions into a profession? Several factors contribute to this challenge:

• Societal norms and preconceived notions that encourage following traditional career paths regardless of personal interests

• Failure to identify and invest in your passions early in life

• Feeling trapped in a current profession, whether financially or otherwise

• Financial and personal commitments that make it difficult to take risks

• Fear of change and reluctance to pursue a less conventional path

• Fear of failure and uncertainty about long-term success

• Lack of acceptance from family, friends, or society when choosing an unconventional career

• Difficulty in identifying a profession that aligns with your passion

Turning Your Passion into Your Profession: Is It Worth Trying?

The answer is a definite yes. After all, you only live once, and it is up to you to ensure you live life to the fullest. Instead of settling for a tedious job that merely pays the bills, why miss out on the thrill and excitement of pursuing your passions? The saying goes, "Love what you do, and do what you love." Turning your passions into your profession allows you to embrace that mindset.

Pursuing your passion enables you to take something you love and care deeply about and transform it into a source of financial stability and personal fulfillment. Moreover, when you align your passion with your profession, you naturally attract like-minded individuals who share your vision, creating a powerful and motivated team.

Overcoming Challenges in Aligning Passion with Profession

A profession fueled by passion turns challenges into stepping stones for growth rather than insurmountable obstacles. The long hours, demanding projects, or steep learning curves become exciting rather than burdensome because they are part of a more extraordinary journey in which you are fully invested. Passion drives perseverance, motivating you to strive for excellence, push through obstacles, and continually improve. Instead of counting the hours until the weekend, you find fulfillment in every milestone and accomplishment.

Reflecting on my journey of aligning passion with profession, I consider myself fortunate. Throughout my career—from teaching and research to corporate roles and eventually entrepreneurship—I have had the opportunity to choose paths that matched my passion for innovation and creation. However, this does not mean the journey was without difficulties. Despite being able to make career choices, there were times when the alignment between my passion and profession was not perfect. I had to navigate the realities of each job and find creative ways to integrate my passion into my professional responsibilities.

One of the most significant misalignments between my profession and my passion occurred early in my career. After completing my studies, I began working as a lecturer at an engineering college. While teaching was fulfilling and allowed me to continue learning and growing, my true passion lay in product development—creating new technologies and solutions that could impact people's lives. However, in the late 1980s, product innovation and entrepreneurship were not as widely encouraged as today. Opportunities for innovation were limited, and engineering education primarily focused on theoretical foundations rather than practical applications.

At that time, my role as a lecturer felt distant from the creative and innovative work that fueled my passion. The teaching system was rigid, primarily focused on preparing students for exams rather than encouraging new ideas or groundbreaking projects. While I could guide final-year students through their project work, there was little room to introduce topics like innovation or entrepreneurship. It felt as though my passion was sidelined, and I struggled to see how I could integrate my love for product creation into a traditional academic environment.

However, during moments of misalignment, we must think creatively about incorporating our passions into our work. Although the system did not directly support innovation, I found small opportunities to carve out space for product development. I began guiding students on final-year projects, encouraging them to choose topics that allowed for creativity and innovation. Even though these were still student-level projects, they represented a step toward aligning my passion with my teaching responsibilities.

One of the most pivotal moments came when I sought opportunities beyond the classroom. I discovered that some industries were open to collaborating with educational institutions, particularly as automation gained traction in the late '80s and early '90s. This growing interest in automation allowed me to align my passion with real-world needs. I realized I could involve my students by forming a small group of enthusiasts who shared my interest in product development. Together, we began working on small industrial automation projects, and that's when the spark returned.

I established a small electronics hobby club with my students, inviting those particularly interested in product development to join. We approached local industries—rubber manufacturing, textiles, and process-based industries—to explore their needs. By immersing ourselves in these industrial environments, we identified opportunities for innovation. One of our first successful projects was designing an automation system for a rubber production line. We developed a machine to automate the cutting of fabric, a process that had previously been done manually. This project allowed us to solve a real-world problem while staying true to our shared passion for innovation.

These collaborations with local industries proved to be a turning point. They provided a practical platform for me to pursue product development while fulfilling my teaching responsibilities. The students gained invaluable hands-on experience, and I found ways to bridge the gap between my passion and my profession. These moments reaffirmed my belief that there are always creative ways to blend the two, no matter how misaligned your profession and passion may seem.

As my career evolved, I encountered similar challenges in different roles. When I transitioned to corporate jobs, the scale was different, but the essence of the challenge remained the same. Corporate life often required me to focus on immediate goals, such as meeting deadlines, managing budgets, and optimizing operations—tasks that sometimes felt far removed from my passion for innovation. However, I learned that even in these environments, opportunities existed to integrate my creative drive into my work.

In corporate roles, the key to aligning passion with profession was identifying areas where creativity and innovation could add value to the business. Initially, these opportunities were not always obvious, and I had to immerse myself in each situation to understand where my strengths could be applied. Whether streamlining a process or developing a new product line, I sought to infuse my passion for innovation into my work. It wasn't about ignoring the professional demands of the job; it was about finding synergies where my passion could enhance my performance and contribute to the company's success.

One of the most critical lessons I learned during these years was the importance of persistence and open-mindedness. Aligning passion with profession isn't always straightforward. In many cases, you must spend time deeply understanding your environment before recognizing opportunities for alignment. It requires patience and a willingness to explore new ideas. You must also be open to learning from every experience, even those that don't seem directly related to your passion at first glance.

For example, when I entered entrepreneurship, I assumed the /alignment between my passion and profession would happen naturally. After all, as an entrepreneur, you have the freedom to create and innovate. But even here, challenges emerged. Running a business involves numerous responsibilities—financial management, marketing, operations—that can sometimes feel disconnected from the core of your passion.

However, I realized the key was approaching every business aspect with the same innovative mindset. Whether working on product development or solving logistical issues, I saw each task as an opportunity to bring my passion to the forefront.

Aligning your profession with your passion is a continuous process that requires creativity, persistence, and flexibility. There will be obstacles along the way, but those challenges can often lead to the most meaningful opportunities for growth. I have integrated my passion for creating new things into every career phase by staying open to new possibilities and finding innovative solutions. Whether through teaching, corporate roles, or entrepreneurship, the alignment may not have always been perfect, but it has always been possible with the right mindset and determination.

Discovering Your Professional Passion

Finding one's professional passion can often feel like an elusive journey filled with uncertainty, self-doubt, and occasional inspiration. Pursuing a career that aligns with our true passions can seem daunting in a world that constantly pushes us to conform to established paths. Yet, this journey is worthwhile and essential for achieving fulfillment and satisfaction in our work lives. Drawing from personal experiences and insights, I present a framework highlighting the importance of immersion, perseverance, and self-exploration in discovering your professional passion.

Understanding Immersion: The Heart of Passion Discovery

Immersion is the cornerstone of finding your professional passion. This concept involves fully engaging with the activities or fields you believe might ignite your enthusiasm. It is not enough to merely speculate about what you might enjoy; you must actively participate in those interests. Think of immersion as an experiment where you test your hypotheses about what excites you through hands-on experience.

You can explore its nuances when you immerse yourself in a particular field. For instance, if you think you might enjoy playing the violin, you must spend time learning the instrument, despite the initial awkwardness of producing "funny sounds." This discomfort is part of the learning curve, and it is crucial to recognize that every expert was once a beginner. Whether it's music, painting, coding, or entrepreneurship, the early stages will likely be challenging.

I recall my initial foray into public speaking. I was terrified of standing before an audience, fearing judgment and failure. However, I decided to immerse myself in the process by attending workshops and participating in community events. The first few speeches were nerve-wracking, and my delivery was shaky. Yet, the more I practiced, the more comfortable I became. Eventually, I found joy in sharing my ideas and connecting with others. Immersion helped me realize that public speaking was not just a skill I wanted to acquire but a passion I wished to nurture.

The Role of Perseverance

Immersion, while essential, is only part of the equation. Perseverance is the fuel that keeps the journey alive, especially when challenges arise. Many people abandon pursuits at the first sign of difficulty, but persistence is key, whether learning an instrument, mastering a new language, or starting a business.

Consider the example of learning to play a musical instrument. Many aspiring musicians quit after just a few lessons, frustrated by their lack of immediate progress. However, those who push through the early struggles develop their skills and gain a deep appreciation for the art. Similarly, individuals who stay committed to any professional endeavor are far more likely to discover and cultivate their passion.

Finding Motivation

Setting small, achievable goals can be highly beneficial for sustaining perseverance. For example, rather than aiming to master an entire piece of music, focus on learning just a few measures. Celebrating these small victories builds momentum and motivation to keep moving forward. Over time, as you reach these milestones, your confidence will grow, making the journey toward your passion more fulfilling.

Spending Quality Time on Your Passion

In today's fast-paced world, skimming the surface of interests is tempting without fully engaging with them. However, dedicating quality time to activities that resonate with you is crucial. This investment allows you to gain deeper insights into what you truly enjoy.

Take a moment to reflect: How often do you set aside uninterrupted time to explore your interests? Some of my most profound insights about my passions have emerged during these dedicated moments. Whether reading, practicing, or networking, allocating focused time to your passion can lead to significant revelations.

The 10,000-Hour Rule

Malcolm Gladwell popularized the idea that it takes approximately 10,000 hours of practice to master any field. While this number is often debated, the underlying principle remains: investing time is crucial to truly understanding your passion. As you spend more time immersed in an activity, you uncover its technical aspects and the emotional connections and motivations that drive your interest.

Reflecting on Your Experiences

As you navigate your journey of immersion and practice, reflection is essential. Taking the time to assess your experiences can clarify whether a particular path genuinely resonates with you. After immersing yourself in an activity for a while, ask yourself the following questions:

• What aspects of this activity do I enjoy the most?

• What challenges have I faced, and how did I overcome them?

• Do I feel excited when engaging in this activity, or does it feel like a chore?

• What skills have I developed, and how do they align with my goals?

These reflections will help you determine whether what you initially believed to be your passion truly aligns with your interests and values.

Seeking Guidance and Community

In discovering your professional passion, consider seeking guidance from mentors or joining communities that share your interests. Connecting with others passionate about similar pursuits can provide invaluable insights and support. They may share their own experiences of challenges and triumphs, inspiring you to persist in your journey.

For example, if you are interested in writing, joining a local writers' group or an online community can expose you to diverse perspectives and constructive feedback. Engaging with others in your field can also lead to networking opportunities and collaborations, further enriching your experience.

Embracing Flexibility and Open-Mindedness

As you immerse yourself in different activities and explore your passions, it is essential to remain open-minded and adaptable. Your journey may not follow a linear path, and that's completely normal. You may start with a particular interest only to discover that your true passion lies elsewhere. This realization is not a failure but simply part of the exploration process.

Embracing a growth mindset allows you to see every experience as a learning opportunity. If a particular pursuit no longer excites you, pivoting and exploring something new is perfectly okay. This flexibility can lead to unexpected discoveries and opportunities that align more closely with your authentic self.

Navigating Financial and Societal Pressures in Pursuing Passion-Driven Careers

First and foremost, it is essential to acknowledge that financial sustainability is crucial when considering a passion-driven career. However, this does not mean abandoning your dreams or sidelining your passions. Instead, it requires a balanced approach that allows you to explore your interests while ensuring financial stability for yourself and your loved ones.

Finding the Balance Between Passion and Profession

The first step is to assess your situation realistically. Are you currently working a job that pays the bills but leaves you unfulfilled? If so, evaluating how you can carve out space for your passion within your current lifestyle is essential. For many, pursuing their dreams does not require an immediate leap into a new career. Instead, it may involve dedicating evenings or weekends to exploring their interests through classes, participating in community activities, or simply practicing a craft they love.

For example, musicians or artists may hold day jobs in fields that seem unrelated to their creative pursuits. However, they often dedicate their free time to honing their craft, joining clubs, or collaborating with like-minded peers. While their daily jobs provide financial stability, their passion fuels their spirit and creativity. This duality does not diminish their commitment to their profession or passion; rather, it enriches their lives by allowing them to engage with both aspects.

One of the beautiful things about passion is that it can be integrated into various areas of life. It can make work more enjoyable and fulfilling, even if it is not directly related to one's primary profession. For example, an accountant passionate about photography might find joy in documenting company events or taking professional portraits of colleagues. This overlap creates a more fulfilling work experience while ensuring that the passion remains an active part of life, rather than fading into the background.

The Importance of Commitment

A significant factor in overcoming societal pressures is commitment to one's passion. This commitment is not merely a fleeting enthusiasm; it requires dedication and perseverance. Many people abandon their dreams in pursuit of materialistic benefits or due to the pressures of maintaining a conventional lifestyle. However, before making such a decision, it is essential to ask yourself: Am I genuinely passionate about this pursuit, or is it merely an infatuation sparked by seeing someone else succeed?

The reality is that passion alone is not enough to guarantee success. It requires hard work, resilience, and continuous effort. Those who have pursued their dreams often share stories of late nights, early mornings, and countless hours spent perfecting their craft. Passionate individuals are typically driven by an internal motivation that transcends societal expectations. They embrace challenges and setbacks as part of the journey rather than as insurmountable obstacles.

If you are hesitant about pursuing your passion due to external pressures, take the time to immerse yourself in it. Engaging fully with your interest can help you determine whether it is a genuine passion worth pursuing. Spend time participating in activities related to your passion—take classes, volunteer, or join communities with similar interests. Through this engagement, you will understand what pursuing this passion entails and whether you are willing to put in the necessary effort to succeed.

Overcoming Excuses and Self-Doubt

When people doubt their ability to pursue a passion-driven career, they often come up with excuses: "I don't have enough time," "I don't have the resources," or "What will others think?" While these concerns are valid, they often stem from a fear of failure or the unknown. Recognizing these excuses for what they are is the first step to overcoming them.

If you frequently make excuses, take a moment to reflect on whether your hesitation is genuinely due to external circumstances or if it arises from self-doubt. It's easy to blame financial constraints or societal pressures when, in reality, the root cause might be a lack of belief in your capabilities. Consider seeking mentorship or connecting with individuals who have successfully navigated similar journeys. Their insights can provide clarity and inspire you to confront your fears head-on.

As you contemplate the pursuit of a passion-driven career, it's crucial to develop a plan. Identify the steps you need to take to transition from where you are to where you want to be. This may include setting short-term goals, such as dedicating a few hours each week to your passion, or seeking opportunities to turn your hobby into a side business. Gradually, as you gain experience and confidence, you can explore how to make your passion a central part of your life.

Financial Considerations and Long-Term Planning

While pursuing your passion, it is essential to consider financial factors. Transitioning from a stable job to a passion-driven career requires careful planning. Creating a financial buffer can provide peace of mind, allowing you to experiment and explore your passion without the immediate pressure of earning a full income. This cushion allows you to focus on your goals without the added stress of financial insecurity.

Consider starting small. Many successful entrepreneurs and artists began their journeys while maintaining their day jobs. They used their evenings and weekends to build portfolios, connect with potential clients, or develop their products. This approach lets you test the waters and see if your passion can evolve into a sustainable career without jeopardizing your financial stability.

Embracing Societal Norms While Staying True to Yourself

Societal pressures can be daunting, especially when they dictate what constitutes a "successful" career. However, it is essential to recognize that everyone's path is unique. While traditional careers may be highly valued by society, pursuing a passion-driven career can be just as valid and fulfilling.

Surround yourself with supportive individuals who understand your journey. Seek out communities that celebrate creativity and passion. Engage with those who have chosen unconventional paths and learn from their experiences. These connections can provide encouragement, motivation, and valuable insights as you navigate your journey.

Moreover, it challenges the narrative that equates success solely with financial gain. Success can be defined in many ways, including personal fulfillment, creative expression, and positively impacting others. Your passion can lead you to a unique definition of success that aligns with your values and aspirations.

Pursuing a passion-driven career amidst financial and societal pressures is challenging but achievable. It requires self-reflection, commitment, and the willingness to face fears and uncertainties. You can confidently navigate this complex landscape by integrating your passion into your current lifestyle, overcoming excuses, and planning for financial sustainability.

Pursuing your passion is about building a career and creating a more fulfilling life. Aligning your work with what you love will enhance your well-being and inspire those around you to follow their dreams. Embrace the challenge, leap, and allow your passions to guide you toward a future that resonates with your true self.

The Harmony of Passion and Profession

At its core, the connection between passion and profession is not just about finding a job that aligns with personal interests; it's about weaving those interests into the fabric of our professional lives. For many, keeping passion separate from profession may seem practical, offering stability and security. However, as I have learned, this separation is often only temporary. Over time, the yearning to pursue what truly excites and motivates us becomes too powerful to ignore.

When I embarked on my career as an engineer, I initially focused solely on the technical aspects of my work, striving for excellence in my field. Yet, I felt a persistent urge to make a meaningful impact beyond the confines of my job description. I soon realized that aligning my passion for social change with my profession would enrich my work and enhance my sense of purpose.

Finding the Overlap: Bridging Passion with Professional Goals

A pivotal moment in my journey was recognizing the potential to integrate my passion for social impact into my engineering work. My technical skills could be leveraged to develop solutions that address pressing societal challenges. By embracing this intersection, I discovered that my expertise could contribute to healthcare innovations that make a tangible difference in people's lives.

This transition was not instantaneous—it required deep reflection and a willingness to explore various avenues. I sought opportunities to engage with healthcare professionals, understand their challenges, and explore how technology could bridge gaps in service delivery. This journey led me to develop affordable healthcare solutions that brought essential services directly to those in need, particularly in underserved communities.

I also taught and mentored others through this process, sharing my knowledge and insights with colleagues and interns. This role allowed me to cultivate the next generation of formal or informal professionals while reinforcing my passion for education. The respect and gratitude I received from students and peers fueled my enthusiasm, reaffirming that aligning passion with profession creates a cycle of mutual growth and enrichment.

The Power of Impact: Making a Difference through Passionate Work

Aligning my passion with my profession has significantly enhanced my overall well-being. I am satisfied to know that my work contributes positively to society. Engaging with healthcare professionals and understanding their needs empowered me to create impactful systems, such as telemedicine solutions in ophthalmology and nephrology.

These innovations have provided healthcare access to individuals who might otherwise be deprived of it, demonstrating how passion-driven work can lead to meaningful change. Witnessing the tangible effects of my efforts—seeing patients receive care through mobile applications regardless of their location—was a transformative experience. It reinforced my belief that the potential for impact becomes limitless when passion meets purpose.

Moreover, the fulfillment derived from making a difference extends beyond professional success. It instills a sense of pride and joy in everyday tasks, transforming work from a monotonous obligation into a source of inspiration. This shift in perspective has improved my mental and emotional well-being, allowing me to approach challenges with resilience and optimism.

Creating a Meaningful Work Environment

Aligning passion with profession has significantly contributed to a more enriching work environment. When individuals integrate their passions into their careers, they become more engaged and motivated. This heightened enthusiasm creates a positive ripple effect, inspiring colleagues and fostering collaboration.

In my experience, this alignment has cultivated a culture of creativity and innovation within my teams. When employees feel empowered to pursue their passions, they are likelier to share ideas, take risks, and push the boundaries of what's possible. This collaborative spirit enhances productivity while strengthening team members' sense of belonging and camaraderie.

The respect and appreciation from colleagues for bringing passion into the workplace have solidified relationships and fostered a supportive atmosphere. When individuals feel valued for their contributions, overall job satisfaction and well-being improve. This synergy between personal fulfillment and professional collaboration creates a vibrant workplace where everyone thrives.

Adapting to Challenges: Resilience through Passion

Aligning passion with profession is not without its challenges. Moments of doubt, obstacles, and setbacks can test one's resolve. However, passion is a powerful source of resilience, driving perseverance through difficulties.

For instance, developing telemedicine solutions required navigating complex regulatory frameworks and technical challenges. During these trying times, my passion for providing accessible healthcare fueled my determination to find innovative solutions. The vision of bridging gaps in healthcare accessibility served as a guiding light, enabling me to overcome hurdles that might have otherwise discouraged me.

Moreover, the alignment of passion and profession has instilled a growth mindset, allowing me to view challenges as opportunities for learning and improvement. This mindset fosters adaptability, enabling me to approach problems creatively and seek solutions that align with my values and objectives.

The Personal Transformation: A Journey Toward Fulfillment

The fulfillment derived from engaging in meaningful work has permeated every aspect of my life, influencing my relationships, outlook, and overall happiness.

I have cultivated a deeper understanding of my values and purpose by embracing my passion for social impact. This clarity has empowered me to make choices that resonate with my authentic self, leading to a more balanced and fulfilling life. I enjoy my professional achievements, the connections I forge, the knowledge I share, and the impact I create.

Ultimately, aligning passion with profession is a continuous journey that requires introspection, openness, and a willingness to adapt. As we navigate the complexities of our careers, we must remain receptive to opportunities for integration. This alignment fosters personal well-being and satisfaction while contributing to a more compassionate and engaged society. Before diving headfirst into a passion-driven career, it's important to debunk some common myths.

Common Misconceptions About Passion-Driven Careers

When we think of passion-driven careers, we often imagine someone who has found their calling and lives in complete alignment with their work and purpose. The notion is romanticized—people doing what they love, waking up enthusiastically every morning, and feeling deeply fulfilled. While this sounds like a dream come true, many misconceptions cloud our understanding of what it truly means to pursue a career based on passion. These myths can be misleading and sometimes demotivating, preventing people from fully embracing the realities of building a passion-driven career.

Misconception #1: You Need Connections or "Godfathers" to Succeed

One of the biggest misconceptions about passion-driven careers, especially in fields like acting or other highly competitive industries, is that success is impossible without connections or influential mentors, often called "godfathers." There's a widespread belief that making it big, particularly in glamorous professions like film or music, requires knowing the right people or employing unethical strategies to get ahead.

However, this view overlooks the importance of perseverance, talent, and hard work. While certain connections may open doors, they do not guarantee long-term success or fulfillment. The key lies in honing your craft and improving your skills. I've known individuals who entered the film industry without privileged backgrounds or influential connections. What they had was perseverance and talent—qualities that eventually enabled them to rise in the industry.

The idea that success requires a shortcut or a helping hand undermines the genuine effort to cultivate one's passion and turn it into a profession.

Passion alone is not enough; it must be supported by consistent hard work, practice, and persistence. Success comes to those who show up consistently, improve over time, and remain focused on their goals, regardless of their starting point.

Misconception #2: Passion-Driven Careers Are Always Glamorous

Another common myth is that pursuing a career in something you love will automatically lead to a life of glamour, excitement, and ease. People often associate passion-driven careers with an idealized version of work—one where every day is thrilling, and challenges feel insignificant because of the inherent joy of doing what you love.

In reality, even the most fulfilling careers have their ups and downs. No matter how aligned your work is with your passion, every profession involves routine tasks, challenges, and moments of doubt. For example, you may be passionate about the automobile industry and dream of designing groundbreaking vehicles. However, once you immerse yourself in the field, you may realize that a significant portion of the work involves long hours, detailed testing, and constant problem-solving. While these aspects may seem less glamorous, they are necessary to achieve the breakthroughs that fuel your passion.

Passion-driven careers require perseverance through the mundane and the difficult. Being passionate about something doesn't mean every work moment will feel magical. There will be setbacks, long hours, and stress. Your commitment is the real test of passion, even when the work feels tedious or overwhelming.

Misconception #3: Passion Always Equals Profession

Many people assume that once they discover their passion, it will seamlessly translate into a profession. This misconception can lead to disappointment when they realize that not all passions are easily monetizable or when the realities of an industry do not match their expectations.

Consider someone passionate about hands-on mechanical engineering. During college, they may have enjoyed building Formula One cars or working on environmentally friendly automotive projects. However, after graduation, they may find themselves in a finance or consulting role, analyzing data rather than engaging in the technical aspects of engineering that they love. Over time, they might question their career choice, feeling disillusioned and distanced from their true passion.

It's important to understand that passion and profession do not always align perfectly. Sometimes, what you enjoy doing in your free time may not translate directly into a sustainable career. That doesn't mean your passion is irrelevant. Instead, you may need to find ways to integrate it into your life through side projects, hobbies, or volunteering, while pursuing a profession that complements your skills and provides financial stability.

Misconception #4: Passion Is a Fixed Destination

One of the more subtle misconceptions about passion-driven careers is the idea that passion is a fixed, unchanging entity. Many believe that once they discover their passion, it will remain constant throughout their lives, and they will always feel the same excitement and drive.

The reality, however, is that passion is fluid and can evolve. As you grow and gain more experience, your interests may shift, and what once excited you may no longer hold the same appeal. This is not a failure but a natural progression of personal development. Sometimes, immersion in a field reveals that what you thought was your passion is not genuinely fulfilling in the long term—and that's perfectly okay.

A career change or pivot is not an admission of defeat; it's a sign of growth. I've seen many professionals start their careers passionate about one field, only to discover a new passion later. For example, an engineer might fall in love with finance or business analysis after initially believing their path lay in mechanical engineering. These discoveries often come after deep immersion in a field and can lead to new, exciting professional directions.

Misconception #5: Passion Alone Is Enough to Sustain a Career

There's a common belief that passion alone can sustain a career. People often think, "If I love what I do, the money will follow." While passion is a powerful motivator, it is not the sole ingredient for a successful and sustainable career. Practical considerations—such as market demand, financial viability, and the necessary skill set—must also be considered.

Many individuals fall into the trap of assuming that just because they are passionate about something, they will automatically excel at it and build a career around it. However, passion must be paired with hard work, continuous learning, and a willingness to adapt. Market realities dictate that passion alone is not enough; it must evolve into something in demand, or one may need to acquire additional skills to turn it into a profession.

For example, if you're passionate about writing, simply enjoying the craft is not enough to build a successful career. You must also understand the business side of writing, including marketing, networking, and possibly self-publishing. Passion is the spark, but success requires strategy, effort, and adaptability.

Rather than seeing passion as a guarantee of success, view it as a guiding force—a compass that helps you navigate your career decisions. But remember, passion alone is insufficient. It must be paired with perseverance, adaptability, and a willingness to learn at every stage of the journey. Only then can you build a career that fulfills your passions while supporting your personal and professional growth. Creating a culture that nurtures passion is not just a personal effort; it must also be systemic.

Fostering Passion-Aligned Work in Industries and Workplaces

As organizations evolve, there is a growing recognition of the need to create environments that foster passion-aligned work. This approach benefits individual employees and the organization, as passionate employees tend to be more engaged, productive, and innovative.

The Role of Leadership in Encouraging Passion

Leadership plays a crucial role in fostering an environment where passion-aligned work thrives. Implementing processes like design thinking is not enough; leaders must also cultivate a culture that encourages employees to pursue their interests. This involves creating space for exploration, supporting continuous learning, and allowing for failure and iteration—key components of design thinking and passion-driven work.

Industries that embrace these principles often have leaders who act as facilitators rather than just managers. They understand that passion cannot be forced—it must be nurtured. A passionate leader is essential because they set the tone for the entire organization. When the leadership team is driven by purpose and enthusiasm, it creates a ripple effect, inspiring others to find and pursue their passions within their roles.

Leaders must also recognize that fostering passion is not a one-size-fits-all endeavor. Just as different users have varied needs in a product design process, employees have diverse passions and motivators. Some thrive on creativity and innovation, while others find fulfillment in problem-solving or helping others. Understanding these differences is key to building an inclusive environment where employees can align their passions with their work.

Design Thinking: A Human-Centered Approach to Passion-Aligned Work

One emerging approach that supports this alignment is design thinking. Design thinking is a human-centered methodology that places the user at the center of the problem-solving process. It encourages empathy, creativity, and iteration, making it an effective tool for product development and creating work environments where employees' passions can flourish.

Traditionally associated with product innovation, design thinking has found broader applications in the modern workplace, where the "user" can be the employee. Since design thinking revolves around understanding the end user's needs, companies can apply the same principles to comprehend and cater to their employees' passions and motivations.

Imagine designing a smart TV where the user's needs are paramount. The design team would conduct thorough research, interview users to understand their requirements, and prototype solutions based on those insights. Similarly, organizations can implement a process of continuous feedback and adaptation to ensure employees work in environments that ignite their passions.

For instance, when designing a TV for elderly users, one might consider their specific challenges, such as cognitive decline or physical limitations. The same principle applies to work environments, where companies must understand what motivates their employees and what barriers prevent them from pursuing passion-driven work. Organizations can create more engaging and supportive workplaces by keeping the "user", in this case, the employee, at the center.

The Five Stages of the Design Thinking Process

Industries can benefit from the structured yet flexible design thinking methodology when creating environments that foster passion-aligned work. This approach emphasizes understanding human needs and generating innovative solutions, making it applicable to product design and workplace culture. The five stages of the design thinking process, developed by the Hasso Plattner Institute of Design at Stanford (d.school), offer a roadmap for building passion-driven environments.

a. Empathize: The first stage focuses on understanding the "users"—in this case, the employees. This step involves observing, engaging with, and comprehending their needs, motivations, and challenges. Employers can cultivate a deep sense of empathy to create conditions that allow employees to connect their passions with their work responsibilities. Empathy is the foundation of passion-driven workplaces, as it fosters an understanding of what drives employees and how best to support their growth.

b. Define: After gathering insights during the Empathize stage, the next step is to define the core problems or opportunities for aligning passion with work. This involves synthesizing the collected information and identifying key barriers that prevent employees from engaging in passion-driven work. As in product development, framing the problem from the employee's perspective is crucial. For instance, instead of stating, "We need to improve employee retention," a more effective approach would be, "Employees need opportunities to explore their passions and feel valued." This shift in perspective helps develop solutions that directly address real needs, fostering a more engaging and fulfilling work environment.

c. Ideate: The third stage is all about generating creative solutions. Organizations should brainstorm and explore various ways to create an environment that nurtures employees' passions. Ideation encourages thinking outside the box and challenging assumptions. Leaders can involve employees in this process, fostering a culture of co-creation where everyone has a voice in shaping the workplace. By empowering employees to suggest ways to make their work more fulfilling, companies can develop innovative solutions tailored to their workforce's needs.

d. Prototype: Once ideas have been generated, it's time to transform them into tangible solutions. The Prototype stage involves developing small-scale, low-cost versions of potential solutions. For example, a company might pilot a program allowing employees to dedicate a portion of their workweek to passion projects or community service initiatives. Prototyping enables organizations to test different approaches, gather feedback, and refine their strategies. The key is experimenting with various models until a viable solution emerges, enabling employees to engage in passion-aligned work.

e. Test: In the final stage, companies test their prototypes by implementing them on a larger scale and collecting feedback. This step is crucial for refining the solution and ensuring it effectively meets employees' needs. Testing may uncover new insights or challenges, prompting companies to revisit earlier stages of the design thinking process. This iterative approach fosters continuous improvement, ensuring that the workplace evolves to support passion and engagement over time.

Although the design thinking process is often described in five linear stages, it is inherently flexible and iterative. Stages can overlap, coincide, or be revisited based on new learnings obtained through testing. This adaptability is essential in cultivating a workplace culture where passion can thrive. As employees' needs and motivations evolve, so must the solutions designed to support them.

The non-linear nature of design thinking mirrors the fluidity of passion. As passions shift and develop, so must the work environments that nurture them. By fostering a culture of continuous improvement and adaptability, organizations can remain responsive to their employees' evolving passions, ultimately creating a thriving workplace.

This approach benefits not only individual employees but also organizations as a whole. Passionate employees tend to be more engaged, creative, and committed. Passion fuels innovation, drives progress, and leads to long-term success, especially in today's dynamic industries.

Usability Engineering: Ensuring Designs Work in Practice

Alongside design thinking, Usability Engineering is another critical discipline that ensures solutions are usable and accessible. It takes a structured approach to improving the user experience of interactive systems, drawing from both computer science and psychology to identify and address usability issues early in the design and development process.

Usability engineering began gaining prominence in the 1980s, with pioneers such as John Whiteside and John Bennett advocating for its principles. The field was further advanced by usability expert Jakob Nielsen, whose 1993 book Usability Engineering outlined techniques for testing and refining designs at multiple stages.

Unlike UX or interaction designers, usability engineers focus primarily on the research phase. Before implementing a product, they identify potential barriers to learnability, efficiency, memorability, error-free use, and subjective satisfaction. Their role is essential in ensuring that the final product resonates with users and meets all necessary usability criteria.

This process involves testing designs with real users or usability experts at various stages. By catching and addressing user experience issues early on, usability engineering reduces the risk of failure at launch and significantly enhances user satisfaction.

Sketching: The First Step Toward User-Centered Design

Sketching is a crucial design tool that bridges usability engineering and design thinking. It provides a simple yet powerful way to propose, explore, and communicate ideas, allowing designers to iterate on multiple concepts before investing time and resources in prototypes or final designs.

The unique advantages of sketching include:

• **Quick:** Sketches can be created in a short amount of time.

• **Cheap:** They require minimal investment and resources.

• **Disposable:** They are easy to discard and iterate upon.

Unlike prototyping, which tests specific functionalities, sketches are used in the early ideation stages when broad concepts are explored. Once the design is refined, usability engineering methods can be applied to ensure it meets all relevant requirements.

By incorporating usability engineering throughout the design process and using sketching as an early tool to explore possibilities, we ensure that the final design is innovative and user-friendly.

The Complementary Nature of Design Thinking and Usability Engineering

Both design thinking and usability engineering emphasize iteration and feedback loops, but they serve different roles:

• Design thinking helps identify the right design.

• Usability engineering ensures that the design is done right.

These two approaches complement each other, guiding the process from exploration to refinement and ensuring innovative and practical solutions.

Organizations can create solutions that effectively meet users' needs by integrating both methodologies. While design thinking allows teams to explore various directions, usability engineering ensures those directions are functional and efficient. This balanced approach results in products that look good on paper and perform seamlessly in users' hands.

Passion in the Workplace: Beyond Entrepreneurship

A common misconception is that passion is only relevant to entrepreneurs. While entrepreneurship often demands a deep sense of purpose, passion is equally important for employees in all roles. It is the driving force that can transform an ordinary job into a deeply fulfilling one.

It's also important to note that passion doesn't have to align perfectly with one's job title. In many cases, passion manifests in specific projects or initiatives within the workplace.

For example, an engineer passionate about sustainability might find fulfillment in working on environmentally friendly projects, even if sustainability isn't their primary job function. A finance professional passionate about storytelling may use those skills in internal communications or branding initiatives.

Companies create a sense of purpose and engagement by allowing employees to pursue projects that align with their interests, leading to higher job satisfaction and retention.

The Power of Passion in Work

When passion and profession align, creativity flourishes. Employees are more likely to think outside the box, explore new ideas, and push boundaries. When people deeply care about their work, they naturally seek ways to innovate and improve. This intrinsic motivation drives personal growth and enhances organizational and industry contributions.

Passionate professionals often:

• Drive change

• Inspire others

• Leave lasting impacts in their fields

Beyond professional success, working in a career that aligns with passion also improves overall well-being. Studies show people passionate about their work experience have lower stress levels and greater life satisfaction. They wake up with a sense of purpose, leading to better mental and emotional health. Their work doesn't drain them—it fuels them, creating a positive cycle of energy and motivation. In the end, aligning passion and profession is a lifelong journey, not a one-time event.

Aligning Passion with Profession: The Journey

Of course, aligning passion with career doesn't always happen overnight. It often requires:

• **Introspection** – Understanding what excites and motivates you

• **Risk-taking** – Being willing to step outside your comfort zone

• **Adaptability** – Finding ways to incorporate passion into your existing role or making a bold career shift

But the rewards are worth it. Whether integrating your interests into your current role or making a career transition, the journey toward merging passion with profession leads to a more meaningful and fulfilling life.

The Ultimate Question: What Would It Take?

As you reflect on your career path, consider:

• What would it take for you to wake up on Monday morning excited for the week ahead?

• How can you infuse more of what you love into your work?

• What steps can you take to turn your passion into a profession?

Pursuing a career that aligns with your passion opens the door to a more satisfying, motivated, and impactful professional life. It transforms Monday mornings from something to dread into something to look forward to.

6

BALANCING VALUES AND REALITY

"Values are like fingerprints. Nobody's is the same, but you leave 'em all over everything you do."

— Elvis Presley

It's Monday morning, the coffee is strong, and you're ready to tackle the week. But even before you hit "reply" on your first email, a stream of decisions and micro-decisions tugs at your values. Did you speak up about that questionable shortcut someone suggested in last week's meeting? Should you push back on a client's request that doesn't sit right with you? For many, the tension between ethical ideals and professional ambitions can feel like walking a tightrope in a whirlwind.

The modern workplace is a bustling arena where new choices are made every day, often placing self-interest and personal ethics on opposite sides of the scale.

These ethical dilemmas are far from abstract; they are the everyday heartbeat of the workplace, made even more complex by the relentless push for growth, efficiency, and profit. And it's tempting, oh, so tempting—to cut corners or bend the rules to climb the corporate ladder or land that big account. Yet, while these shortcuts may seem appealing, they come at a cost. Short-lived gains often backfire, chipping away at the trust we've built with colleagues, clients, and, most importantly, ourselves. Because, as it turns out, making values-based decisions doesn't just make us feel good—it builds self-respect, fosters genuine relationships, and creates lasting trust with those we serve and work with.

But how do we walk this talk in the real world? How can we make the most of our professional lives without compromising our principles? The answer lies in creating what I call "the authentic brand"—a professional identity built on integrity, admired for consistency, remembered for standing firm on values, and, above all, trusted. Authenticity is a rare and powerful currency in a world saturated with polished images and corporate promises. By aligning our actions with our principles, we create a foundation that holds up under pressure and stands the test of time.

This chapter will explore practical strategies for embedding values into decision-making without sacrificing ambition. We'll examine real-life examples and tackle common ethical dilemmas in the workplace, demonstrating how staying true to your principles can coexist with—and even fuel—professional success. The goal is to inspire a vision of deeply fulfilling, sustainable, and impactful success—a career where you're not just advancing but thriving, grounded in values you can stand by every step of the way.

In the 1990s, I was in an unexpected dilemma between professional ambition and my values. This period marked a time of intense growth for me as both a teacher and a learner in engineering education. I started as a lecturer at SJCE Engineering College in Mysore before transitioning to the MS Ramaiah Institute of Technology in Bangalore as a student officer. Teaching was not merely a job for me—it was a calling. Every morning, I stood in the classroom, pouring my heart into my lectures, committed to providing the best education possible for my students. But, as life often does, it presented a challenge that tested my principles, work ethic, and perception of the teacher's role in society.

During those years, I balanced my teaching duties with consultation work for companies, applying engineering principles to real-world challenges. As my reputation as an educator grew, I noticed a growing demand for additional lessons, particularly from students outside my college who needed extra guidance to succeed in their engineering courses. Despite my already rigorous schedule, I couldn't ignore this need. These students approached me with genuine eagerness, seeking clarity on subjects crucial to their careers. Many traveled from towns across Karnataka—from places like Hubli, Chikmagalur, and Ramanagaram—after hearing about my teaching style and accessibility. I felt a deep sense of responsibility to support them, but doing so meant adding even more to my workload.

This is how my foray into private tuition began. The work was both challenging and fulfilling—I witnessed students from various colleges make significant strides in their understanding and saw firsthand the impact of this extra support on their lives. Yet, despite the positive results, doubts crept in. By offering private tuition, was I weakening the existing educational system? Was I inadvertently creating an alternative to the structured education colleges and universities provided? I grappled with these questions, recognizing that while helping students gain valuable knowledge, I also charged a fee for my sessions. Financially, it benefited me, but I knew this endeavor was about more than just income.

Around this time, I sought advice from one of my mentors, Mr. Kamath, an accomplished electrical engineer and successful entrepreneur. Having studied in the U.S. and returned to India, he dedicated his later years to teaching young professionals about ethics and responsibility—qualities I deeply admired. I trusted that his guidance would provide an unbiased perspective.

After hearing my dilemma, he offered wise counsel: "If your teachings enable students to overcome barriers and complete their degrees, then you support them meaningfully." His insight helped me see my tuition work in a new light. I wasn't merely providing an educational service but contributing to a much-needed support system in our academic landscape.

Mr. Kamath suggested an approach that allowed me to reconcile my values with my professional activities. He advised me to consider the diversity of the students I served—some could afford the tuition, while others struggled financially. "Why not," he proposed, "create a balance by offering free or reduced fees for those from less privileged backgrounds?"

This idea gave me clarity. Implementing a flexible model allowed me to expand my reach without compromising my integrity. It allowed me to serve as a bridge for students across different socioeconomic backgrounds, uniting them in their common pursuit of knowledge. For those who could afford it, the tuition was a nominal fee for my time and expertise. For students with limited means, I subsidized the cost or taught them at no charge. This approach helped me maintain fairness while ensuring no student was denied learning due to financial constraints.

My journey through this dilemma taught me that there is rarely a perfect answer to complex decisions. Sometimes, the best solution is to strike a balance that aligns with our core values while accommodating the realities of the situation. The experience made me keenly aware of how easy it is to become paralyzed by the fear of "doing something wrong," to the point where one risks doing nothing. Had I not offered tuition, hundreds of students would have missed the opportunity for additional guidance. I would have limited my impact to the fifty or so students in my classroom rather than reaching a much broader group from different towns and backgrounds.

Looking back, my education and consultation work and my commitment to ethical conduct helped me evolve as a professional. By staying true to my core values of knowledge-sharing and equality in education, I found peace with the choices I had to make. This arrangement allowed me to support my family and advance in my career while remaining grounded in the purpose I believed in: empowering young minds. It taught me the importance of flexibility and creating a path forward, even if it meant bending traditional rules slightly to ensure a positive outcome.

This experience serves as a reminder that every professional will inevitably encounter crossroads that require a realignment of values. These situations force us to consider what we truly stand for and where our non-negotiable boundaries lie. My journey highlighted the importance of integrity, compassion, and adaptability. Yes, there were compromises along the way, but they were made consciously, without violating the essence of my ethics.

Today, I refer to this experience whenever I face another difficult decision. My commitment to my core values has only deepened, and my approach to problem-solving has been enriched by the realization that solutions sometimes lie in the grey areas of life. As professionals, we are not immune to dilemmas or moral challenges. How we approach them matters most—with a clear purpose and an unwavering commitment to our ethical foundation.

How Values Shape Decisions

Values are more than abstract principles; they are the foundation we build our lives and careers. Reflecting on my professional journey, I realize that my values have been the compass guiding my decisions, shaping my path in ways I could not have anticipated. They are deeply rooted in my upbringing and were significantly influenced by my father, a clerk in the gold mines. His unwavering commitment to integrity and diligence profoundly impacted my approach to work and life.

My father's philosophy was simple yet profound: "If I am working for someone, I should do my best, regardless of what I am earning." He instilled in me the belief that hard work and integrity are paramount, regardless of the circumstances or rewards. Growing up, I witnessed his rise from a second-division clerk to an accounts officer through sheer determination and dedication. His ascent was not just about career advancement—it was a testament to the strength of his values.

I recall times when senior executives, including the mines' CFO, sought my father's counsel on critical issues. They respected him for his impartial thinking and ability to confront uncomfortable truths. He never hesitated to speak up when something was wrong, always advocating for what was right. His steadfast adherence to his values allowed him to navigate the complexities of his workplace with grace and honor.

During those formative years, I absorbed these lessons without fully realizing the profound impact they would have on my career. I learned that values should be guidelines and lived principles we embody daily. This perspective became crucial as I entered the professional world, where challenges often blur ethical lines, and the temptation to compromise one's values can be significant.

As I ventured into engineering education and consultancy, I found that my father's teachings echoed my decisions. I firmly believed that when faced with dilemmas, I needed to evaluate them through the lens of my value system. Instead of being swayed by fleeting emotions or external pressures, I would step back and ask myself: Does this decision align with my core beliefs? Is it within the purview of my principles? This reflection has guided me repeatedly, ensuring that my choices resonate with who I am and what I stand for.

In the early stages of my career, I established a vision statement that encapsulated my values and ambitions. A strong value system should be clear, precise, and easily understood, as a guiding star for every individual within a team or organization. Lofty ideals alone weren't enough; they needed to translate into actionable principles that employees could embrace and embody.

While at the MS Ramaiah Institute of Technology, I applied these principles by fostering a culture of integrity and excellence among my students and colleagues. I encouraged open communication, transparency, and accountability, creating an environment where everyone felt empowered to voice their opinions and contribute to the common good. This approach wasn't just about achieving academic success but building character and instilling a sense of responsibility toward society.

As I progressed in my professional journey, I recognized that our responsibilities extend beyond our immediate tasks. We are all part of a larger ecosystem, interconnected with our communities and the environment. This realization deepened my commitment to giving back to society, a fundamental aspect of my value system. My father's example of working diligently while striving to contribute positively to his community resonated with me, inspiring me to seek ways to make a difference.

How Values Shape Decision-Making

Values are crucial in shaping our decisions, influencing our choices, and how we approach various situations. Here's how values guide decision-making:

• **Guiding Principles** – Values serve as a framework for evaluating options, helping individuals determine what is most important to them. They provide a foundation for making choices that align with their beliefs and priorities.

• **Clarity in Priorities** – Strong values help clarify what matters most when faced with multiple options. For example, someone who values honesty may prioritize transparency in their decisions, while another who values security might choose options that minimize risk, even if it means forgoing potential rewards.

• **Influencing Behavior** – Values shape behavior by influencing how individuals respond to situations. A person who values teamwork may actively seek collaboration and input from others, while someone who values independence might prefer to work alone.

- **Conflict Resolution** – Values act as a moral compass in conflict or ethical dilemmas. Individuals reflect on their values to navigate tough decisions, ensuring their choices align with their principles.

- **Long-Term Goals** – Values shape aspirations and career paths. People are more likely to pursue work, relationships, and projects that resonate with their core beliefs, leading to greater satisfaction and fulfillment.

- **Cultural and Social Influences** – Cultural, social, and familial influences shape values. When individuals make decisions, they often consider how their choices reflect their upbringing, community norms, and societal expectations.

- **Emotional Resonance** – Decisions aligned with one's values evoke positive emotions and a sense of integrity. Conversely, choices that contradict deeply held beliefs can lead to guilt, regret, or dissatisfaction, reinforcing the importance of staying true to one's principles.

- **Adaptation and Growth** – Values can evolve based on experiences and personal growth. As individuals gain new insights, their decision-making may shift, allowing them to adapt to new circumstances while remaining grounded in their core beliefs.

By integrating values into decision-making, we ensure that our choices are not just reactive but intentional, shaping a path that aligns with our sense of purpose and integrity.

Values are fundamental to decision-making. They serve as a compass, guiding choices, shaping behaviors, and influencing overall life satisfaction. By helping individuals navigate complexities and align their actions with their authentic selves, values ultimately contribute to a sense of purpose and direction.

One of my core values is the belief that professionals are responsible for uplifting those around them. This principle guided my decision-making when developing educational programs and initiatives. I sought opportunities to provide mentorship, support underprivileged students, and create knowledge-sharing platforms. The goal was to equip individuals with skills and empower them to contribute positively to society.

For instance, when students approached me for guidance outside of regular classes, I could have easily turned them away, citing time constraints or focusing solely on my official duties. Instead, I embraced these requests, understanding that each interaction was an opportunity to impact a student's life. By offering additional tuition, I wasn't merely enhancing their academic performance—I was fostering a sense of community, demonstrating the importance of shared learning, and fulfilling a societal obligation to support those in need.

However, this path was not without its challenges. I often grappled with balancing my professional commitments with my desire to assist struggling students. Was it ethical to charge tuition fees, or would that contradict my values of accessibility and support? I was at a crossroads, facing a decision that tested my commitment to my principles.

In those moments of uncertainty, I drew upon my father's wisdom. He had always emphasized that while values should guide us, they should allow flexibility without compromising integrity. With this in mind, I devised a system that offered discounted rates for students from less privileged backgrounds while maintaining a fair pricing structure for others. This approach enabled me to uphold my commitment to education while sustaining my professional efforts.

The realization that my professional success should not come at the expense of my values was a turning point. I began to see my career not merely as a means to an end but as a platform to fulfill my commitment to society. Each decision became an opportunity to align my actions with my principles, reinforcing the belief that one can succeed while making a meaningful impact.

The influence of my values extended beyond individual decisions—they shaped the culture of the teams I built and the organizations I was part of. I actively promoted a workplace environment of ethical behavior, collaboration, and mutual respect. This culture enhanced productivity and fostered a sense of belonging, where employees felt valued and inspired to contribute their best. A truly successful organization is one where everyone understands their role in serving the greater good.

These experiences have deepened my appreciation for the intricate relationship between values and professional decisions. Values are the bedrock of our identity, guiding us through adversity and uncertainty. They compel us to act with integrity, seek opportunities to uplift others, and contribute positively to our communities.

Today, as I continue my journey in education and consultancy, I remain committed to the principles instilled in me by my father. His example reminds me of the importance of integrity and hard work, shaping my professional choices and definition of success. For me, success is not merely measured by financial gain or career advancement—it is about the legacy we leave behind, the lives we touch, and the impact we create.

My values serve as a beacon of hope in a world often driven by competition and self-interest. They remind me that our professional lives can be a force for good and that we can pursue our passions while remaining steadfast in our commitment to integrity and social responsibility. This alignment between values and actions fosters a sense of fulfillment that transcends conventional notions of success, reinforcing the belief that we are all stewards of our communities.

Reflecting on my journey, I see how deeply intertwined my values are with my professional decisions. They have shaped my career and the lives of those around me, creating a ripple effect of positive change. I encourage everyone to reflect on their values and consider how they can guide their professional paths, fostering a culture of integrity, collaboration, and service. We can make a meaningful difference by aligning our values with our actions, one decision at a time.

Role Models of Integrity – Leaders Who Embody Commitment to Values

In modern business, where profit often overshadows principle, it is refreshing to encounter leaders who remain steadfast in their commitment to ethical values. These individuals inspire their teams and redefine what it means to lead with integrity. I deeply admire three leaders: Narayan Murthy, Dr. Venkateswamy, and Dr. Mashelkar. Their unwavering dedication to their values has shaped their respective organizations and the communities they serve, offering invaluable lessons for those striving to make a meaningful impact in their professional lives.

Narayan Murthy: A Beacon of Ethical Leadership

Narayan Murthy, the co-founder of Infosys, is an exemplary figure in ethical leadership. His business philosophy blends ethics with inclusivity, emphasizing that success should never come at the cost of moral integrity. Murthy's guiding principle—"leave and let live"—advocates for a business model that benefits shareholders, employees, customers, and society.

Infosys stands as a testament to this ethos. It is not just a globally successful IT company but a platform that has created multiple billionaires among its employees and stakeholders. This achievement is particularly remarkable compared to other major corporations that often prioritize profit over people. Under Murthy's leadership, Infosys fostered a culture of collaboration and shared success, proving that a company can thrive while uplifting those who contribute to its journey.

What truly sets Murthy apart is his commitment to recognizing the contributions of all employees, regardless of their role. In an industry where high-ranking executives often receive the spotlight, Murthy made headlines by ensuring that even his long-serving driver and cook received shares in the company. This act of kindness reflects his deeply rooted values and underscores the importance of recognizing the human element within business operations. By making wealth creation inclusive, Murthy has set a gold standard for ethical leadership that strongly resonates with my principles.

Dr. Venkateswamy: Transforming Healthcare Through Compassion

Another leader I deeply admire is Dr. Venkateswamy, the visionary founder of Aravind Eye Hospital. His approach to healthcare embodies a profound commitment to serving the underserved, a principle that holds immense significance in today's world of increasing inequality. Under his leadership, Aravind has grown into the largest eye care hospital in the world, proving that healthcare can be both accessible and sustainable.

Dr. Venkateswamy understood that financial barriers often prevent those in need from receiving critical medical services. In response, he pioneered an innovative cross-subsidization model, where paying patients help cover treatment costs for those who cannot afford it. This model ensures high-quality care for all patients and allows the hospital to operate sustainably. By treating one paying patient, the hospital can subsidize care for two free patients, creating a scalable, self-sustaining system that challenges traditional healthcare delivery models.

What inspires me most about Dr. Venkateswamy is his unwavering dedication to making healthcare accessible to all, particularly those from rural and disadvantaged backgrounds. He didn't just build a hospital—he created a movement centered on compassion and equity. His work demonstrates how strong values can seamlessly integrate into business models, leading to financial success and significant social impact.

At a time when many healthcare systems are plagued by bureaucracy and rising costs, Dr. Venkateswamy's visionary philosophy serves as a beacon of hope. His approach exemplifies how empathy and service can transform industries, challenging us to think creatively about how we can address societal issues within our respective fields.

Dr. Raghunath Mashelkar: A Visionary for Scientific Integrity

The third leader who inspires me is Dr. Raghunath Mashelkar, a renowned scientist and former Director General of the Council of Scientific and Industrial Research (CSIR) in India. Dr. Mashelkar's journey—from humble beginnings to a position of global influence—exemplifies the power of perseverance and dedication to societal advancement. His commitment to preserving the integrity of

India's rich scientific heritage is commendable, especially in an era where intellectual property rights often favor wealthier nations.

Dr. Mashelkar identified critical vulnerabilities within India's patenting landscape, where foreign corporations frequently sought to exploit the country's traditional knowledge and resources. He took significant steps to protect indigenous knowledge and advocate for innovation that benefits society. One of his most notable contributions was his advocacy for a patent system that honors nature's creations, preventing foreign entities from patenting traditional Indian herbs and medicinal resources with minor modifications.

His work strengthening India's patenting system reflects his deep commitment to equity and fairness. By ensuring that India safeguards its indigenous innovations, Dr. Mashelkar has elevated the country's status in global research and inspired future generations of scientists to innovate ethically and sustainably.

What inspires me most about Dr. Mashelkar is his emphasis on giving back to society. He firmly believes that scientists are responsible for using their knowledge for the greater good, a philosophy that deeply aligns with my values. His work encourages us to leverage our skills and expertise to address pressing societal challenges, reinforcing that true success is measured by personal achievements and the positive global impact we create.

The Collective Impact of Values-Based Leadership

The common thread that binds these three leaders—Narayan Murthy, Dr. Venkateswamy, and Dr. Mashelkar—is their unwavering commitment to their values, which they have seamlessly integrated into their professional journeys. Their stories serve as powerful reminders that ethical leadership is not just an aspirational ideal but a practical and effective approach that yields remarkable results for organizations and society.

Their influence extends far beyond their respective fields. They challenge us to reflect on our values and consider how they shape our decisions. Each of these leaders embodies the idea that when we lead with integrity and prioritize the well-being of others, we create an environment where collaboration, innovation, and compassion can flourish.

Murthy, Venkateswamy, and Mashelkar's examples inspire a different narrative—one that emphasizes shared success and collective responsibility. They remind us that business and ethics are not mutually exclusive; instead, they can coexist harmoniously, driving both sustainable growth and societal advancement.

I carry these lessons, striving to embody the values these leaders exemplify. Their commitment to integrity, service, and knowledge-sharing resonates deeply with my aspirations, guiding me to make choices that reflect my values in my work and interactions.

The Consequences of Letting Go of Values

Values define who we are. They shape our decisions, influence our relationships, and guide us through life's complex landscape. But what happens when someone abandons these core principles—the very foundation of their identity? The repercussions are often profound, extending far beyond the initial decision and affecting every aspect of personal and professional life.

• The Initial Temptation: The Lure of Short-Term Gains

It often begins with temptation—an enticing opportunity that promises an immediate reward. Perhaps it's a lucrative business deal that requires an ethical compromise, or a career promotion that demands overlooking harmful practices. In these moments, the appeal of immediate success can overshadow the inner compass that once guided decisions. The allure of such gains can be influential, convincing individuals that temporarily setting aside their values is a justifiable means to a desirable end.

• The Short-Lived High: The Thrill of Success Without Integrity

The initial compromise often brings an intoxicating thrill—a sense of achievement, recognition, or financial gain. However, this euphoria is short-lived. Beneath the surface lies a growing tension between who they once were and who they are becoming. This internal dissonance breeds stress, anxiety, and guilt, slowly eroding the sense of fulfillment that comes from authentic success. While the emotional toll may not be immediately evident, it overshadows any short-term achievement over time, leaving an individual feeling hollow rather than fulfilled.

• The Erosion of Trust: Losing Credibility in Other's Eyes

One of the most significant consequences of abandoning one's values is the loss of trust, both self-trust and the trust of others. Trust is the foundation of personal and professional relationships, built on mutual respect and honesty.

When values are compromised, the damage extends beyond reputation, undermining credibility with colleagues, clients, and loved ones. Rebuilding trust can take years, if it can be rebuilt at all. Others may begin to question the authenticity and reliability of those who have abandoned their principles, often leading to isolation, diminished influence, and fractured relationships.

• The Weight of Regret: The Emotional Toll of Compromise

As time passes, the thrill of short-term gains is often overshadowed by regret. Upon reflecting on past decisions, individuals may realize the actual cost of their choices—lost opportunities for genuine connections, moments of authenticity, and the satisfaction of a life that aligns with their beliefs.

Regret can manifest as guilt, shame, or a pervasive sense of failure, creating a heavy emotional burden that affects mental health and overall well-being. It can lead to sleepless nights, chronic stress, and a lingering feeling of unfulfilled potential. Regret is a powerful force—one that, if left unaddressed, can profoundly impact both personal and professional life.

• Identity Crisis: Losing Sight of Who You Are

When core values are abandoned, individuals often experience an identity crisis. For many, values are deeply intertwined with their sense of self, shaping how they perceive themselves and wish to be perceived by others. Letting go of these guiding principles creates confusion and disconnection, leading individuals to question their identity.

This search for meaning becomes even more challenging without a moral compass, leaving them adrift, unable to navigate life's complexities with clarity or confidence. As a result, they may struggle to reconnect with their true selves, finding it difficult to regain a sense of purpose and direction.

• The Ripple Effect: How Compromise Affects Others

When someone compromises their values, the consequences extend far beyond the individual. These effects ripple outward, impacting friends, family, colleagues, and communities.

Such behavior can create a toxic culture in the workplace, where unethical practices become normalized, placing pressure on others to conform. The change can strain relationships among family and friends, altering dynamics and leading to disappointment or distrust.

Value compromises within organizations erode trust, respect, and integrity, ultimately harming collaboration and fostering an environment where individuals prioritize self-interest over collective goals.

Accountability as a Foundation for Sustainable Success

Accountability must become a foundational element of business practices to counteract the trend of compromising values for expediency. Organizations can establish clear ethical guidelines and cultivate a culture prioritizing integrity over short-term profits.

Ethical leadership plays a crucial role in this transformation. Leaders who model honesty and transparency inspire others to uphold similar values. Furthermore, training programs on ethical decision-making empower employees to navigate difficult situations without compromising their principles, fostering an environment where integrity is non-negotiable.

Building Ethical Resilience: A Shift Toward Long-Term Fulfillment

Consumers and investors can also support this shift by engaging with businesses that commit to ethical practices. Socially responsible investing and conscious consumerism reflect a growing demand for organizations to align with moral values, reinforcing the belief that ethics and profitability coexist. This movement presents an opportunity for companies and individuals to redefine success, not as short-term achievements but as sustainable growth grounded in integrity and social impact.

Real-World Consequences: Lessons from High-Profile Figures

High-profile cases illustrate the dangers of abandoning values for short-term gain. Take the example of businessman Vijay Mallya, who was once celebrated as a symbol of India's entrepreneurial success. Mallya's ambition drove him to expand his family's business, Kingfisher, beyond the liquor industry, venturing into airlines and sports. But in pursuit of rapid growth, he made reckless decisions, over-leveraging and mismanaging resources, and resorting to questionable financial tactics. This departure from ethical decision-making led to severe legal and financial troubles, resulting in the downfall of his empire and a tarnished legacy of betrayal and disappointment.

Another cautionary tale involves the collapse of several chit-fund companies, particularly in regions like Bangalore. These schemes promised unrealistic returns, enticing people to seek quick profits. However, the founders' desire to expand rapidly led them to cut corners, masking financial mismanagement.

When funds ran dry, many founders disappeared with investors' money, leaving countless families devastated and instilling a pervasive distrust in investment opportunities. Such cases reveal a systemic issue: the dangers of prioritizing short-term gains over ethics and integrity, which ultimately harm entire communities.

The Rise and Fall of Saravana Bhavan's Founder

One of the most significant examples of ethical compromise leading to a tragic downfall is the story of Saravana Bhavan's founder, P. Rajagopal. Saravana Bhavan, an iconic South Indian restaurant chain, rose to international fame for its vegetarian cuisine, establishing numerous branches worldwide. Rajagopal built an empire, drawing attention for his business acumen. However, this success came at a high cost; Rajagopal's actions led to one of India's most publicized criminal cases, tainting his business legacy.

Rajagopal's journey illustrates how a person can be admired for professional success and condemned for personal transgressions. He became entangled in legal trouble due to his involvement in a disturbing murder case, pursuing actions that contradicted ethical and legal standards. Despite his wealth and influence, Rajagopal's deeds could not shield him from justice; he was ultimately convicted and spent the remainder of his life in prison, where he passed away. His case underscores the dangers of abandoning moral standards, as his unethical choices tarnished the brand he worked so hard to build. Saravana Bhavan remains a successful brand, yet Rajagopal's actions are a haunting reminder of the potential consequences of placing personal desires above ethical values.

Kingfisher Airlines: Vijay Mallya's Empire Built on Unstable Ground

Vijay Mallya's story is equally cautionary, embodying the risks of aggressive, high-stakes business tactics without a stable ethical foundation. Known as the "King of Good Times," Mallya was celebrated for his flamboyant lifestyle, ownership of Kingfisher Airlines, and prominent status in India's business and social spheres. His ventures spanned from the airline industry to ownership in the Indian Premier League (IPL) and Formula One, amplifying his reputation as a successful entrepreneur. However, behind the scenes, financial and ethical mismanagement contributed to the collapse of his empire. Kingfisher Airlines was launched with fanfare, quickly becoming a major player in India's aviation market. Yet, the business's financials were built on a shaky foundation, with mounting debts and a reliance on aggressive borrowing. As financial strains escalated, Mallya's use of funds from Indian banks, intended for airline operations, was scrutinized. Allegations arose that Mallya redirected these funds to personal accounts and overseas investments, contributing to the airline's eventual grounding. By 2013, Kingfisher Airlines was defunct, and Mallya faced mounting legal challenges in India. In 2016, Mallya fled to the UK, avoiding Indian authorities and leaving unpaid debts totaling over ₹9,000 crores owed to Indian banks. His life of luxury contrasted sharply with the legal and financial chaos left in his wake. Now, he is remembered less as a business magnate and more as an economic fugitive, with multiple extradition requests and ongoing legal proceedings that have yet to be resolved. Mallya's story is a powerful lesson in the importance of transparency, financial responsibility, and ethical accountability, showing how failure to uphold these values can dismantle even the most impressive empires.

The Nirav Modi Scandal: Fraud on an International Scale

The case of Nirav Modi is another compelling example of how short-term gains through unethical practices can lead to long-term repercussions. Nirav Modi was a prominent jeweler and diamond merchant known internationally for his luxury jewelry brand and celebrity endorsements. However, beneath the veneer of glamour, Modi orchestrated one of the largest banking frauds in Indian history, deceiving the Punjab National Bank (PNB) and other financial institutions in a scam worth over ₹14,000 crores.

Modi fraudulently secured massive bank loans using fake Letters of Undertaking (LoUs). By exploiting loopholes in the banking system, he diverted funds for business expansion into personal assets and luxury items. When the scheme was uncovered, Modi fled India, following a similar path to Mallya. His actions resulted in severe financial strain for PNB and shook public confidence in the Indian banking system.

Today, Modi faces extradition efforts as authorities continue to seize assets linked to the fraudulent transactions. The once-celebrated jeweler, admired for his craftsmanship, now symbolizes corruption and deceit in the business world. His case exemplifies the destructive nature of greed, showing how individuals willing to compromise principles for profit ultimately pay a steep price. Moreover, Modi's actions impacted countless stakeholders, from investors to employees, eroded trust in institutions that took years to rebuild.

Mehul Choksi and the Gitanjali Gems Collapse

Closely associated with Nirav Modi and Mehul Choksi, the former Gitanjali Gems owner faced a similar downfall. Like Modi, Choksi was involved in the PNB scam, leveraging fraudulent Loans to obtain loans and misusing funds for personal gains. Together, the Modi-Choksi duo orchestrated a scam that exploited gaps in regulatory oversight, exposing vulnerabilities in India's banking sector.

Choksi fled to Antigua and Barbuda, securing citizenship before Indian authorities could detain him. Despite repeated attempts by the Indian government to extradite him, Choksi remains outside India's jurisdiction. His actions damaged his reputation and caused massive losses for banks and investors. The Gitanjali Gems brand, once a trusted name in Indian jewelry, now symbolizes betrayal and fraud.

The impact of the PNB scam extended beyond the immediate financial losses. It exposed regulatory weaknesses and prompted tighter scrutiny within the banking industry, sparking debates about accountability and the need for stronger safeguards. Choksi's fall from grace underscores the broader implications of unethical practices, illustrating how a few can destabilize an entire sector and erode public trust.

Systemic Impact: Political and Corporate Corruption

Beyond individual cases, we see similar ethical failures in business and politics, where leaders make decisions based on personal gain rather than the public good. Scandals involving bribery, nepotism, and corruption degrade trust in institutions, fostering widespread disillusionment. In societies where such practices become the norm, businesses may feel compelled to engage in unethical behavior to stay competitive. This normalization of unethical actions can create a cycle where values are easily sacrificed, eroding social trust and slowing progress toward a more equitable society.

Creating a Culture of Consistent Ethical Reinforcement

Embedding values at the start of an employee's tenure is only the beginning; companies must continuously reinforce these principles to sustain an ethical culture. At Tata, performance evaluations go beyond measuring business achievements—they also assess alignment with the company's ethical standards.

Tata's annual performance reviews include clear guidelines for evaluating each employee's adherence to ethical principles, reinforcing that integrity is just as important as productivity. Employees are held accountable for their work results and for upholding the company's core values.

Strict policies and immediate consequences for ethical violations strengthen this value-driven culture. Tata maintains a zero-tolerance policy—employees found compromising ethical guidelines face immediate dismissal. This unambiguous stance underscores the company's commitment to ethical integrity at every level, reinforcing that values are non-negotiable.

Empowering Employees Through Ethical Decision-Making Tools

Providing employees with the resources and skills to navigate ethical dilemmas is crucial for fostering a culture of integrity. Many companies struggle with ensuring consistent ethical decision-making because employees feel unprepared or unsupported in challenging situations.

To address this challenge, Tata has developed a structured decision-making model featuring hypothetical scenarios and possible responses aligned with the company's values. This framework equips employees with practical tools to make confident, ethically sound decisions even in high-stakes situations.

By integrating ethical decision-making into daily business operations, Tata ensures that employees view ethics as a habit rather than a burden. Over time, this approach reinforces a culture where employees feel empowered and trusted to make decisions that uphold the organization's principles.

Ensuring Value-Driven Leadership at Every Level

Leadership plays a pivotal role in setting an organization's ethical tone. At Tata, senior managers undergo rigorous ethical training through the Tata Business Excellence Model (TBEM), a guiding framework designed to strengthen ethical decision-making at the highest levels.

TBEM is particularly critical when leaders face strategic decisions such as mergers, acquisitions, and partnerships. By applying this framework, Tata ensures that ethics precedes short-term gains, reinforcing a long-term commitment to values-based leadership.

A strong top-down commitment to ethics sends a powerful message to employees and stakeholders: ethical decisions are the rule, not the exception. When leaders embody company values, they inspire employees to do the same. Seeing senior management make value-driven decisions, even at the expense of immediate profits, reinforces trust and strengthens employees' belief in the company's ethical standards.

This approach transforms the workplace into a supportive environment where ethical decision-making becomes ingrained at every level of the organization.

Encouraging Open Communication and Transparency

A strong ethical foundation requires a culture of openness and transparency, where employees feel comfortable discussing ethical concerns without fear of retaliation.

Companies can promote ethical dialogue by implementing:

• Anonymous reporting systems or whistleblower programs, allowing employees to report unethical behavior discreetly

• Regular ethics workshops and roundtable discussions, where employees can ask questions, seek guidance, and share experiences

• Leadership-led conversations on ethical dilemmas, reinforcing the importance of integrity in everyday decision-making

Transparency should extend beyond internal discussions—companies must also communicate openly with employees and stakeholders about their ethical successes and challenges. Acknowledging achievements and struggles demonstrates a genuine commitment to continuous improvement, fostering trust among employees and the broader business community.

When employees see that a company is honest about its ethical journey, they feel more connected to the organization's mission and are more likely to align their values with those of the company.

Promoting Long-Term Relationships Over Short-Term Gains

One of the biggest challenges in fostering value-driven decision-making is the pressure to achieve short-term financial success. However, businesses prioritizing long-term relationships over immediate profits create sustainable, value-driven cultures that endure.

At Tata, this commitment is evident in employee retention rates, with 70–80% of employees remaining with the company until retirement. This loyalty reflects Tata's values-based culture, where employees feel part of something meaningful and enduring rather than just another cog in the corporate machine.

By encouraging long-term relationships with employees, customers, and stakeholders, companies build a network of trust and goodwill that pays dividends over time. Organizations committed to values attract like-minded, value-conscious customers, enhancing brand reputation beyond short-term financial gains.

This approach contributes to financial stability while solidifying the company's image as an organization with principles and integrity. It makes the company a preferred choice for customers, investors, and future employees, ensuring its continued success and influence.

Aligning Business Strategy with Ethical Goals

To maintain a value-driven environment, businesses must integrate ethical principles into their strategic goals. This alignment ensures that every business decision, whether operational or strategic, is made with a clear understanding of its ethical implications.

This philosophy is embedded in Tata's approach to new ventures and partnerships. Their Tata Business Excellence Model (TBEM) guides decision-making, ensuring each initiative aligns with the company's core values.

When values are deeply integrated into business strategy, organizations achieve consistency across all departments. Employees across different functions operate under the same ethical framework, making prioritizing ethics in daily tasks easier. Decisions are no longer purely financial—they become opportunities to reinforce the company's commitment to integrity and social responsibility.

Cultivating a Value-Driven Culture

Creating an environment that fosters value-driven decisions requires more than well-crafted policies. It demands a deeply rooted commitment from every level of the organization.

From onboarding to leadership training, from performance reviews to transparent communication, businesses must actively cultivate an ethical culture that aligns with their core values.

Tata's enduring success exemplifies how a strong values-based foundation promotes ethical decision-making while contributing to:

• Long-term employee loyalty

• A culture of trust

• Resilience in the face of challenges

When companies prioritize integrity, they ensure sustainable success beyond profit margins and into the hearts and minds of those they serve.

Strategies for Staying True to Professional Values

Modern professionals face continuous pressures, including competition, technological advancements, and rapid organizational scaling. While these changes drive innovation, they create tensions that challenge individuals to align their actions with their core values.

Remaining anchored in a solid value system is essential in such fast-paced environments. While companies define guiding principles through mission and vision statements, individuals must ensure their daily actions reflect these values.

1. Understanding and Adopting the Company's Value System

One of the first steps in maintaining professional integrity is internalizing the organization's values. In mission and vision statements, businesses outline their broader aspirations and ethical commitments, but these ideals must be translated into everyday actions. Companies often implement structured processes with checks and balances to facilitate this, ensuring that critical functions operate within ethical boundaries. These frameworks help professionals make confident decisions without compromising ethical standards.

However, while corporate guidelines are essential, it is the responsibility of each individual to adopt and embody them in their work. For example, in collaborative settings, a professional should focus on:

• Interacting with colleagues with respect

• Fostering mutual trust and transparency

• Upholding integrity in decision-making

By treating these principles as personal standards, employees help create a unified organizational culture where values are not just words on paper but lived daily.

2. Building Personal Accountability Practices

Accountability is crucial for professionals who want to stay true to their values, especially when not directly supervised. A practical approach to personal accountability is setting weekly or monthly reflection sessions to review recent decisions and assess whether they align with personal and professional principles.

For example, managers might evaluate decisions affecting their team, ensuring they promote inclusivity, fairness, and transparency in their leadership.

Journaling is another effective method for maintaining accountability. By documenting daily actions and reflecting on moments when values might have been compromised, professionals can identify patterns or recurring situations where they tend to veer off course. This self-awareness strengthens one's ability to resist ethical lapses in the future.

3. Developing Clear Boundaries and Recognizing Limits

Establishing clear boundaries is essential for professionals who want to avoid compromising their integrity, particularly in high-pressure environments.

This principle is especially relevant in intense competition, such as sales, finance, and consulting, where professionals often face pressure to meet quotas. The temptation to exaggerate claims or withhold critical information can be strong in these situations.

To stay aligned with ethical standards, professionals must define personal limits and resist actions that undermine their integrity.

Boundaries also extend to workplace interactions. Respecting professional limits in collaboration, leadership, and teamwork fosters a culture that aligns with core values. Violating these boundaries—such as exploiting power dynamics, dismissing others' contributions, or encouraging unfair competition—damages relationships and undermines an organization's ethical foundation.

4. Balancing Innovation with Ethical Responsibility

The modern professional landscape encourages innovation, pushing individuals to think outside the box and challenge conventional norms. However, while innovation drives progress and success, it must be balanced with ethical responsibility.

A disruptive mindset is essential for breakthroughs, but innovation can lead to harmful consequences without ethical considerations.

For example, in the tech industry, companies frequently push the limits of data collection and artificial intelligence, sometimes at the cost of user privacy and security. Professionals in such fields must weigh the risks and ensure that technological advancements do not violate fundamental rights or compromise public trust.

By prioritizing long-term ethical standards, professionals can drive progress responsibly and ensure that innovation serves both business and societal well-being.

5. Embracing Empathy as a Professional Guideline

An empathy-driven mindset is fundamental to maintaining alignment with ethical values. It shifts the focus from personal or organizational gain to considering the broader impact on colleagues, customers, and society.

A simple yet powerful question to guide decision-making is:

• Does this decision benefit others?

• Does it harm anyone?

Empathy is essential for leaders. Leadership decisions directly influence team morale, productivity, and workplace culture. Empathetic leaders are more likely to uplift their teams, creating an environment where ethical decision-making is the norm rather than an exception.

An organization that fosters empathy reduces the likelihood of a toxic work culture, where unethical compromises become commonplace.

6. Continuous Learning and Ethical Training

Staying informed about industry standards, ethical norms, and regulatory requirements is crucial in today's fast-evolving business environment.

Professionals committed to ethical growth should seek ongoing training and resources to refine their understanding of value-based decision-making.

Many organizations offer periodic ethical training sessions to:

• Reinforce company values

• Address emerging ethical dilemmas

• Ensure compliance with updated industry regulations

Beyond formal training, professionals can:

• Seek mentors who embody the values they aspire to uphold

• Study case studies of ethical leadership and value-based organizations

• Engage with thought leaders who prioritize integrity in business

By adopting continuous learning, professionals strengthen their ethical resilience and ensure that principled decision-making remains a core aspect of their career growth.

7. Promoting Transparency and Open Communication

Transparency is the foundation of an ethical workplace culture, reinforcing accountability and trust across all levels of an organization. Open communication—whether in voicing concerns, admitting mistakes, or providing clear justifications for decisions—creates an environment where professionals feel empowered to act according to their values.

When leaders and managers model transparency by explaining the rationale behind their decisions, it sets a precedent for others to follow.

Practical applications of transparency include:

• Disclosing potential conflicts of interest to maintain fairness in decision-making.

• Admitting mistakes openly and working toward solutions rather than covering them up.

• Acknowledging challenges in a project rather than downplaying difficulties.

This kind of openness fosters trust, ensures hidden agendas do not derail ethical commitments, and strengthens an organization's value system.

8. Focusing on Collective, Long-Term Impact Over Short-Term Gains

In high-stakes environments, short-term gains can be tempting but often come at the cost of long-term stability and ethical integrity. Professionals prioritizing the broader, long-term impact are better positioned to maintain ethical consistency, even under pressure.

For example, an executive evaluating cost-cutting measures could invest in sustainable business practices rather than selecting an option that lowers expenses but damages environmental or social responsibility goals.

Although the initial financial return may be lower, this long-term approach:

• Upholds ethical integrity

• Strengthens customer trust

• Resonates with today's values-driven consumers

Customers, employees, and investors support businesses that prioritize sustainability and social responsibility more than ever.

This demonstrates that ethical decisions are not just about morality but also about building a blasting business.

9. Encouraging Feedback and Constructive Criticism

Feedback is a powerful tool for professionals to assess and realign their actions with their values. Encouraging constructive criticism allows professionals to gain insights from colleagues, mentors, and customers, helping them identify blind spots and areas for improvement.

Ways to incorporate feedback into professional growth include:

• Regular performance reviews that evaluate both business outcomes and ethical alignment.

• Open-door policies that invite employees to voice concerns about workplace culture.

• Customer feedback mechanisms to understand whether business practices reflect consumer expectations and values.

A feedback-rich environment does not just highlight mistakes—it reinforces a culture of continuous ethical improvement. When ethical misalignments are addressed constructively rather than punitively, employees become more open to learning and refining their decision-making.

Handling Situations Where Values and Business Decisions Clash

Most difficult negotiations and workplace disputes stem from value conflicts—situations in which core values, ethics, or beliefs seem to conflict with practical business decisions.

Examples of Common Value Conflicts in Business

• Business partners disagree over the ethical standards expected of each other.

• A negotiator refuses to work with a potential partner they view as unethical.

• A company decision prioritizes profit over sustainability, raising ethical concerns.

Value conflicts often escalate because people feel a deep emotional attachment to their beliefs and refuse to make concessions that might appear to compromise their values. However, research shows that value-based conflicts can be resolved by approaching them with the right strategies.

Three Strategies for Negotiating Value-Based Conflicts

1. Find Common Ground Without Compromising Core Values

In value conflicts, it is easy to focus on differences, but it is essential to identify shared priorities. Even when parties disagree on core principles, they may still have common interests.

For example, business partners who disagree on ethical standards might still share the goal of long-term company growth. Finding common ground helps redirect discussions toward mutual benefits rather than a standoff over values.

• Identify overlapping interests in the broader picture.

• Reframe disagreements to focus on shared goals.

• Explore compromises that uphold ethical values while meeting business objectives.

2. Reframe the Conflict as a Problem-Solving Challenge

Instead of treating value-based disagreements as moral battles, consider approaching them as practical challenges that require creative solutions.

For example, if an employee refuses to work with a company due to ethical concerns about sourcing materials, the organization could:

• Explore alternative suppliers that align with their ethical standards.

• Create stricter oversight mechanisms to ensure compliance.

• Develop a corporate social responsibility initiative that balances ethical concerns with business needs.

By framing value conflicts as problem-solving exercises, teams can find solutions that honor ethical commitments without sacrificing business success.

3. Use Perspective-Taking to Foster Mutual Understanding

One of the most effective ways to resolve value-based conflicts is to encourage both parties to see the issue from the other's perspective. This approach fosters empathy and helps de-escalate emotionally charged disputes.

For example, if a negotiator refuses to do business with a client on moral grounds, perspective-taking could help:

• Understand the negotiator's ethical concerns and address them thoughtfully.

• Encourage the negotiator to consider business implications without dismissing their concerns.

• Find middle ground, such as working with the client under specific ethical conditions.

Professionals can depersonalize the conflict by acknowledging the emotions and values behind a disagreement and creating space for rational, values-driven solutions.

Maintaining Your Values in a Professional Landscape

Using third parties or respected external experts for conflict resolution can help maintain professional integrity and values when facing ethical dilemmas. Sometimes, conflicts are best settled in informal settings such as networking events, casual meetings, or even outdoor activities like treks, where discussions can be more open and less adversarial. Patience and professionalism also serve as valuable tools in ensuring consistency in one's values throughout a professional journey.

Future Directions: Integrating Ethical and Impact-Driven Models

Business value systems have historically mirrored political and societal structures, evolving from feudal frameworks centered around hierarchy and control to more democratic, socialistic ideals emphasizing equality, rights, and collective welfare. Modern businesses operate within a capitalist framework where meritocracy, innovation, and profitability take precedence. However, there is a growing shift toward integrating ethical, social, and environmental considerations into business strategy.

This transformation reflects a more profound understanding that success must extend beyond financial metrics to include sustainability, social impact, and ethical governance. The future of business lies in aligning economic success with values that foster long-term societal progress.

From Feudal Hierarchies to Democratic Welfare Models

In pre-industrial economies, business values were closely tied to feudalistic norms. Resources, wealth, and power were controlled by a select few, and businesses primarily existed to reinforce these societal structures. Social mobility was minimal, and individual success was primarily determined by birth and class rather than personal effort or capability. Business operations in this period focused on maintaining stability and serving the needs of the ruling elite.

As societies evolved, particularly in post-colonial contexts like India, democratic and socialist values gained prominence. These frameworks emphasized equal opportunity, social welfare, and collective progress. Access to fundamental needs such as education, healthcare, and housing became recognized as societal responsibilities, leading to policies to uplift historically disadvantaged groups. Welfare-driven initiatives, such as India's reservation system, were implemented to promote inclusivity.

While this model fosters more significant social equity, it challenges business efficiency. Without competition-driven meritocracy, inefficiencies emerged within industries, limiting growth and innovation. Businesses had to balance the need for inclusivity with the practicalities of economic progress.

The Shift to Capitalism: Meritocracy, Innovation, and Profitability

With globalization and economic liberalization, business values transitioned towards a capitalistic model emphasizing individual effort, competition, and market-driven efficiency. Countries like the United States became leading examples of this shift, positioning themselves as hubs of opportunity where businesses recruited top global talent based on skill and merit rather than social background.

This shift fostered innovation, allowing talent to thrive in an environment where success was determined by ingenuity, effort, and strategic thinking. Businesses prioritized growth, profitability, and market expansion, rewarding individuals and organizations that adapted quickly to economic changes.

However, capitalism's focus on financial gain as the primary indicator of success also introduced significant challenges, including:

• Widening social inequalities as wealth is concentrated among a select few.

• Environmental degradation due to profit-driven industrial expansion.

• Short-term decision-making that prioritized immediate gains over sustainable development.

While capitalism fueled economic progress, it also highlighted the need for businesses to adopt more holistic value systems that address ethical concerns alongside financial objectives.

The Emergence of Ethical and Impact-Driven Business Models

As businesses and consumers became more aware of the consequences of unchecked capitalism, a shift toward value-based business practices emerged. This approach integrates financial growth with sustainability, social responsibility, and ethical leadership principles.

Companies today are increasingly expected to:

• Incorporate environmental, social, and governance (ESG) frameworks into their operations.

• Support social impact initiatives that address systemic inequalities.

• Prioritize long-term sustainability over short-term financial gains.

This new business paradigm acknowledges that economic success and societal well-being are not mutually exclusive. Companies that balance profitability with ethical considerations attract loyal customers, dedicated employees, and long-term investors who value sustainability and social impact.

The future of business will not merely be about maximizing shareholder value but fostering stakeholder capitalism, where success is measured by its contribution to employees, communities, and the environment.

The Shift Towards Triple Bottom Line and Sustainable Business Practices

The business value model is shifting once again. Modern capitalism is increasingly embracing corporate social responsibility (CSR) and environmental, social, and governance (ESG) principles, encapsulated by the "triple bottom line" framework. This approach emphasizes three interconnected priorities: profit, people, and the planet. Once considered an idealistic notion, the triple bottom line has successfully aligned businesses with sustainable practices that benefit both shareholders and society.

• **Profit:** While profitability remains a crucial objective, companies now recognize that long-term success extends beyond quarterly earnings. Businesses integrating social and environmental initiatives into their operations achieve financial stability, enhance their public image, build trust, and attract purpose-driven consumers and employees.

• **People:** The traditional shareholder-centric model is evolving into a stakeholder-inclusive approach. Companies increasingly take responsibility for their impact on employees, customers, communities, and society. This shift has led to a stronger focus on fair wages, diversity, inclusion, and positive workplace environments. Additionally, corporate partnerships with nonprofits and community initiatives reinforce a commitment to social impact, making "giving back" a key measure of success.

• **Planet:** Environmental sustainability has become a fundamental component of business ethics. With growing awareness of climate change and environmental degradation, companies are adopting sustainable practices such as reducing emissions, conserving energy, and utilizing eco-friendly materials. Consumers now favor businesses with firm environmental commitments, and investors increasingly prioritize companies with high ESG ratings, linking sustainable practices directly to financial performance.

The triple-bottom-line approach is both a value-driven and practical strategy. Purpose-driven businesses consistently outperform those focused solely on profit. By adopting this framework, companies build long-term resilience, mitigate risks associated with environmental and social challenges, and contribute to global sustainability efforts.

The Future of Business Values: Integrating Ethics, Social Impact, and Sustainability

As businesses evolve, values are expected to become more deeply integrated into corporate decision-making, balancing economic growth with social impact and environmental sustainability. This trajectory suggests several key shifts:

• **Enhanced Social Impact Measurement:** Future businesses will measure success by customer numbers or market share and by their contributions to improving lives and addressing societal needs. Models like Tata's aim to create meaningful touchpoints across economic classes, setting a precedent for people-centered impact. This approach will become a core business strategy, particularly in essential sectors like healthcare and education, where the value of lives impacted can far outweigh financial metrics.

• **Environmental Stewardship:** The environmental impact of business decisions will continue to gain priority. More companies will adopt carbon-neutral or even regenerative business models, moving beyond the goal of "not harm" to actively restoring and rejuvenating ecosystems. Technologies enabling cleaner energy, waste reduction, and sustainable materials will be critical in shaping future value systems. Businesses will increasingly champion environmental ethics throughout their operations and supply chains.

• **Ethical Governance and Accountability:** Transparency and accountability will become fundamental to business values. Companies will recognize that their legal, ethical, and moral responsibilities extend beyond compliance. Ethical practices—such as fair labor policies, transparent reporting, and responsible sourcing—will be essential for maintaining reputation and trust. In an era where consumers are well-informed and corporations are held accountable, integrity in governance will be a key differentiator.

• **Technology and Innovation for Good:** As technology becomes a cornerstone of the modern economy, businesses will explore its potential for positive societal impact. AI-driven solutions that enhance accessibility, innovations in renewable energy, and advancements in digital health will shape business values. Purpose-driven innovation—focused on profitability and social good—will increasingly guide business strategies.

The evolution of business values has transitioned from feudal hierarchies to democratic-socialistic models, through capitalism, and now toward a model that balances profit with social and environmental responsibilities. The contemporary emphasis on the triple bottom line—profit, people, and planet—marks a new era in which success is defined not just by financial performance but also by a company's ability to contribute positively to society and the environment.

Future businesses will thrive by combining financial growth with purpose-driven initiatives that impact the world. This shift reflects a profound realization: Businesses hold the power and responsibility to address some of the world's most pressing challenges. The values shaping tomorrow's businesses will center on ethics, social impact, and environmental stewardship, fostering a model of success that aligns with society's well-being and aspirations.

True success is built on ethical principles, long-term thinking, and a commitment to serving the greater good. By prioritizing values, businesses can cultivate a landscape of trust, transparency, and collaboration. The challenge lies in upholding integrity even in the face of adversity. Only by doing so can we create a society that values ethical behavior and resilience, paving the way for sustainable success and a brighter future for all.

Ultimately, values are not merely abstract ideals—they form the foundation of our existence. They shape decisions, guide relationships, and define our sense of purpose. While abandoning these values may seem tempting in the short term, the consequences can be far-reaching and damaging. We create a path to authenticity, integrity, and fulfillment by embracing and honoring our values. The journey may be challenging, but the rewards of living in alignment with our true selves far outweigh the fleeting appeal of compromise. As we navigate the complexities of life, let us remember: our values are the compass that will always guide us home.

CONCLUSION

Embracing the new era of impactful success

As we reach the end of Transforming Success, let us take a moment to reflect on what lies at the heart of true success in our modern world. No longer defined solely by wealth, prestige, or individual accolades, success today demands something more profound—an alignment with values, empathy, and a purpose beyond self-interest. This book has been an invitation to rethink, redefine, and ultimately transform how we approach personal and professional growth.

Often, we only see the epitome of success—the accomplished entrepreneur, the industry giant, the world-class athlete, or the tireless social activist. Yet, behind every visible triumph lies an untold story of perseverance, sacrifice, and relentless effort. Success is not merely about reaching the pinnacle—it is about the journey, the lessons learned, and the impact left behind.

The traditional view of success has long prioritized individual achievement and financial gain, often overshadowing the broader impact of our actions. However, as explored throughout this book, a more meaningful definition of success embraces collaboration, resilience, and social good. The stories shared here are not just lessons but a call to action—a reminder that our careers can create lasting change, both for ourselves and the world around us.

At the heart of this transformation lies teamwork, an essential force in building something more significant than any individual can achieve alone. In today's interconnected world, where challenges are complex and intertwined, the ability to work cohesively with others has never been more critical. Whether launching an innovation, addressing community needs, or creating opportunities for others, success in this new era demands unity. We must learn to embrace diverse perspectives, recognize the strengths of those around us, and create environments that foster collective excellence.

Equally important is empathy, a quality often sidelined in the pursuit of efficiency or profit. Yet, empathy is not just a soft skill—it is the foundation of effective leadership, a bridge to deeper understanding, and a tool for fostering genuine relationships. Through empathy, we begin to see others not just as colleagues, employees, or customers, but as individuals whose lives we can positively impact. By prioritizing empathy, we cultivate ethical, compassionate workplaces where people feel valued, understood, and supported.

Another core theme has been the importance of discovering and aligning with one's purpose. In a world that encourages constant comparison, measuring our worth against others' achievements is easy. However, true fulfillment comes not from competition but from living in alignment with our values. Purpose elevates our work beyond financial gain, transforming it into a platform for personal growth, contribution, and impact.

Finding a way to integrate passion into our profession is not just a luxury—it is essential. In a world that often demands compromise, crafting a career that excites us and contributes to a greater good provides resilience, motivation, and long-term satisfaction. Passion fuels persistence, enabling us to overcome challenges with conviction. This alignment is the foundation of a fulfilling, sustainable career and a meaningful life.

Beyond passion, we must also recognize the importance of integrity in professional success. The pressures of ambition and achievement can sometimes tempt us away from our core values, but maintaining integrity is the cornerstone of lasting impact and authentic leadership. A career guided by ethical decision-making leads to external success and fosters a legacy of trust, respect, and honor.

Now, as you turn the final pages of this book, the real journey begins. Armed with insights, stories, and a renewed perspective, you have the tools to bring these lessons to life. Every day offers a fresh opportunity to embrace empathy, seek purpose, champion teamwork, and let your values guide your decisions.

Whether you are an entrepreneur, a seasoned professional, or someone considering a new path, remember this: your career has the power to be a force for good. Your choices today can create ripples, touching lives and reshaping communities in ways you may never fully see, but you can take pride in knowing that your impact is real.

Let us build businesses and careers that reflect not just our skills but also our hearts. Let us craft legacies that go beyond financial gain, leaving a mark on others in meaningful ways. As you carry these insights forward, remember: the most remarkable success is not just the one that fulfills you but uplifts the world around you.

Together, let us redefine success for ourselves and future generations—one that is inclusive, impactful, and truly transformative.

ABOUT THE AUTHOR

Dr. Shyam Vasudeva Rao is a distinguished innovator, entrepreneur, and leader in healthcare technology and medical electronics. As the Founder & Director of Forus Health Pvt Ltd., Renalyx Health Systems, and Rx Digi Health Platform, he has pioneered affordable healthcare solutions that have significantly impacted global healthcare accessibility.

His flagship innovation, 3nethra, an all-in-one eye screening device, has won numerous awards, including the DST Lockheed Martin Gold Medal and the Anjani Mashelkar Inclusive Innovation Award. At Renalyx, he spearheaded the development of India's first innovative hemodialysis machine, revolutionizing kidney care and making treatment more accessible and cost-effective.

Dr. Rao's career spans leadership roles at Philips Medical Systems, where he established innovation frameworks and expanded patent portfolios, and at Ericsson, he led R&D and strategic product management. He also serves as Technical Director at Maastricht University, NL, fostering multidisciplinary healthcare and life sciences research.

Under his leadership, over 40 clinicians have pursued advanced research MD-PhDs, creating a new generation of clinician-scientists. This is especially important for value creation in our country, as it fosters an ecosystem for healthcare and life sciences innovation and applied research, while providing a significant boost to the Make in India and Atmanirbhar Bharat missions.

A prolific inventor, Dr. Rao co-created the Knox Card, a hardware-based antivirus solution in 1989. He has filed 25+ international patents, with 20+ India and US patents granted, and has published over 50 technical papers. He also initiated a unique PhD program at Philips to bridge healthcare and technology, fostering indigenous, affordable medical innovation in India.

His contributions have earned him prestigious accolades, including the IoT Thought Leader Award (2016) and the Marico Innovation Award (2017).

Dr. Rao holds a BE Electronics and Communications, Master's in Industrial Electronics from SJCE, Mysore University, and has a research background in High-Performance Computing from the Indian Institute of Science, Bangalore. His work drives innovation in affordable healthcare, making a lasting global impact.

www.ingramcontent.com/pod-product-compliance
Lightning Source LLC
Chambersburg PA
CBHW020606270326
41927CB00005B/200